FOR SUCH A TIME AS THIS

FOR SUCH A TIME AS THIS

*The Arizona Christian University 2021-22
Basketball Season*

Jack Vande Zande

XULON PRESS

Xulon Press
2301 Lucien Way #415
Maitland, FL 32751
407.339.4217
www.xulonpress.com

Contribution by: Jeff Rutter Head Coach

Paperback ISBN-13: 978-1-66287-308-9
Ebook ISBN-13: 978-1-66287-309-6

DEDICATION

This book is dedicated to all the coaches and athletic directors who gave me the opportunity to either coach with or for them since 1990.

Lucky Wurtz, Laconia High School, Rosendale, Wisconsin

Steve Larson, Edgewood College, Madison, Wisconsin

Phil Kamrath, Pardeeville High School, Pardeeville, Wisconsin

Tim Flood, Campbellsport High School, Campbellsport, Wisconsin

Bill Albrecht, West Bend West High School, West Bend, Wisconsin

Joe Pintens, West Bend West High School, West Bend, Wisconsin

Phil Ourada, West Bend East High School, West Bend, Wisconsin

Ryan Tomczyk, West Bend East High School, West Bend, Wisconsin

Kevin Doornek, West Bend East High School, West Bend, Wisconsin

Kyle Fueger, West Bend East High School, West Bend, Wisconsin

Jeff Rutter, Arizona Christian University, Glendale, Arizona

In memory of Henry J. Vande Zande, my father, who introduced me to basketball at a young age.

Thanks to my wife, Carrie, and our children, Ben and Meredith, for the many sacrifices they made for me through the years, which allowed me to coach basketball.

TABLE OF CONTENTS

Introduction
    What Is a Firestorm? ix
Acknowledgments.....................................xv
Foreword..xvii
1   COVID Strikes.....................................1
2   March Sadness 9
3   Meet the 2021–2022 Team 19
4   A Fresh Start......................................55
5   Work Before Play...............................63
6   Time to Get After It............................71
7   Let the Golden State Athletic
    Conference (GSAC) Games
    Begin 95
8   Trip to the Sunshine State for
    Thanksgiving.....................................103
9   It's the Most Wonderful Time
    of the Year...125
10   Cactus Classic 147
11   January Highs and Lows....................165
12   Firestorm Keeps Rolling....................205
13   Championship Finish.........................225

14 National Tournament........................251
15 Kansas City–Bound............................275

Afterthoughts...311
About the Author 321

INTRODUCTION

WHAT IS A FIRESTORM?

When Southwestern College became Arizona Christian University in 2011, the students voted on changing the team name from Eagles to Firestorm. A firestorm is a conflagration which burns so fiercely that it creates and maintains its own windstorm. Firestorm is also a fictional superhero in American comic books. A phoenix bird named Stormin' Norman is the current mascot. Just like a phoenix bird is a mythological bird that was reborn from ashes, so it is with Christians who receive spiritual rebirth as followers of Jesus Christ. Their unique team name truly fits a university with a motto of "Transforming Culture with Truth."

The reason why this book is being written is twofold. First, I always heard how challenging writing a book can be. Being a retired middle school English teacher and someone who has read many sports- and faith-based books, writing a book became a goal of mine in recent years. Second, there are books written about Power Five conference collegiate athletic programs, either about a particular championship team or coach. Reading a book about a successful basketball team at a small private National Association of Intercollegiate Athletics (NAIA) Christian university would be exclusive.

To be honest, I had never heard of Arizona Christian University until 2020, when I applied for the position I currently have with the university. Most small private universities in Wisconsin switched from NAIA to National Collegiate Athletic Association (NCAA Division III) affiliation through the years, so I no longer had an awareness of many NAIA schools. Thankfully, there are still around 230 colleges and universities in the country with the NAIA. The top NAIA basketball programs play at an NCAA Division 1 mid-major level.

Through the years, I had been receiving postings of college basketball coaching openings through the Indeed job site. It just so happened that, in the summer of 2020, Arizona Christian University Men's Basketball program was searching for an assistant coach to join their staff. I called and left a message with Coach Jeff Rutter, and I figured I would not hear back from him. Surprisingly, two hours later, Coach Rutter returned my call. We talked for twenty-five minutes about everything but basketball, and then, the last five minutes, we talked about basketball. Coach Rutter was looking for a mature Christian coach with real-life experiences, who would be comfortable with building relationships with players, sports ministry, and assisting where needed.

When I told Carrie about this call, she was supportive. She knew I had a desire to be an assistant at the college level. We decided to pursue this coaching/ministry opportunity until God put up a stop sign. After lots of prayer and the blessing from our parents and children, we accepted the position.

Our daughter, Meredith, pointed out, "Dad, you have to take this job. It involves sports ministry, basketball, and warm weather. You will regret it if you don't at least try it for a year."

Our son, Ben, chimed in, "This is a perfect retirement job for you."

The stop sign never came up!

In September of 2020, I headed to Arizona to start at ACU. Carrie and her mother moved down during the summer of 2021. It is definitely a "God thing" with how it all worked out.

This book is unique in many ways. It begins with the COVID issues and trying to have a basketball season with the ever-changing time of COVID 2020–2021. Next came the disappointing setback to end the 2020–2021 season. Then, at the beginning of the 2021–2022 season of "Such a Time as This," God placed the team members and coaches at ACU for a memorable season. The title of the book comes from the Old Testament story of Esther. God orchestrated that she would be placed in the position of Queen. Queen Esther had to make a bold stand before the king to save the Israelites from genocide. "And who knows but that you have come to your royal position for such a time as this?" (Esther 4:14).

Scripture is used before every chapter in the book, and each Bible verse ties into the content of that particular chapter. The book will cover preseason workouts, a team retreat, summaries of the games, and some side stories and vignettes. Writing the game summaries was quite natural for me. Prior to becoming a teacher, I worked in radio broadcasting, and I did play-by-play of many basketball games. Referring to the sports information department's play-by-play of the game was crucial with game time and score. Thanks for all the hard work that sports information departments do.

ACKNOWLEDGMENTS

I need to thank Tim Gooszen and the Arizona Christian University Sports Information Department for their work to provide statistics, play-by-play, Coach Rutter's quotations, and photos for this book. Also, thanks to the other Golden State Athletic Conference (GSAC) sports information departments for statistics and quotes.

Without the encouragement from Maureen Furno and her editing and feedback, I am not sure if this book would have been completed.

FOREWORD

Our 2020–2021 season ended abruptly in Lewiston, Idaho, at the hands of Carroll College of Montana. Although we were the higher seed, we were chasing them for most of the game. We fought until the end, but we just hadn't established championship habits that would carry us through this type of game. Each time we got within striking distance, we didn't execute some small detail, and it came back to bite us. As we approached the spring, there was a feeling among our returners that we had unfinished business. It became clear to me that if we were to continue to grow as a program, we had to raise the standard.

We had to develop championship habits that would carry us through a postseason road game like the previous year. We attacked the preseason with a new focus. It did not take long for the guys to buy into this new direction. We were committed to becoming tougher, smarter, and more unselfish, all while focusing on becoming the biblical men God has called us to be.

It was a season of growth and consistent improvement. The team elected to hold each other accountable to behaviors, such as communication, extra work outside of practice, opponent preparation, and arriving early to everything we do so that we would be physically and mentally prepared in all that we did.

The small commitments added up to significant changes. This was a different team. This team was willing to make sacrifices of comfort and personal preferences and was bought into developing habits that would carry us through difficult times.

A few moments stand out when I began to think this team had a chance to be special. In the locker room after a close loss in November at Division 1 Loyola Marymount of Los Angeles, there was a genuine disappointment that we did not pull it out. These guys believed that we were better. A midseason, last-second thriller victory with second-ranked Carroll College of Montana once again proved we were tougher and unshakeable. After a disappointing January loss the night before, we went into nationally ranked William Jessup and ended their thirteen-game winning streak.

This team was different. These guys bought in, became elite defensively, and had an uncommon belief, taking ACU and the basketball program on a magical postseason run that won't soon be forgotten.

—Jeff Rutter
Head Men's Basketball Coach
Arizona Christian University

The 2021–2022 Men's Basketball season provided a unique opportunity for our campus community to come together in support of our Firestorm Men's Basketball program. As the season moved along, we garnered more and more interest from the campus community to see the team in action—enjoying the fast-paced style of play, athletic abilities, and excellence in competition. The games played late in the season had particular meaning as the team inched closer to a conference championship and climbed the national rankings. The Events Center was packed with standing-room-only opportunities for the campus community to see the Firestorm finish the regular season. In all my years at ACU, I have not seen a facility as packed with excited supporters as those games late in the year. It was fun to see our students, pep band, dance and cheer teams, student life groups, faculty and staff, local high school basketball teams, and long-time Firestorm basketball supporters all come together to cheer on the team to a conference championship.

When the team moved into the national tournament, the on-campus community continued its support from afar. "Watch" parties popped up all over campus, with groups of staff and students joining together to watch the Firestorm move through the opening round and into the semifinals. The semifinal game was played on the "big screen" in the Events Center, with hundreds of students, faculty, and staff in attendance to show support for the team. We were all so proud of the Men's Basketball program—coaches, student-athletes, and staff—for representing ACU so well on a national stage, and doing so with professionalism, excellence, and humility.

—Dr. Peter T. Dryer
Director of Athletics and Dean
of Students
Arizona Christian University

CHAPTER 1

COVID STRIKES

"Bless the Lord, O my soul, and forget not all His benefits, who forgives all your iniquity, who heals all your diseases, who redeems your life from pit, who crowns you with steadfast love and mercy" (Psalm 103:2–4).

"Oh, that wasn't so bad," boasted one Arizona Christian University (ACU) basketball player.

"That was the worst experience I ever had in the training room!" complained another player as his eyes watered, and he walked past other members of the team. "Good luck in there, fellas!"

1

Both players had just been tested for COVID by the New Mexico State trainer in the ACU training room a day before the teams would play. New Mexico State had agreed to play an exhibition game at the ACU Events Center in Glendale, Arizona, in late November of 2020. Both teams were looking for preseason contests because it was extremely challenging to get games arranged.

The whole world came to a screeching halt in the spring of 2020 when the COVID pandemic swept across America and the world. Every person was affected by this virus in some way, shape, or form, even with all the precautions that had been taken by the CDC (Center for Disease Control) and the government.

That included all sports at all levels. To the dismay of many basketball fans, March Madness did not happen for the National Collegiate Athletic Association (NCAA), National Association of Intercollegiate Athletics (NAIA), or high school state tournaments. That included the ACU Firestorm

Men's Basketball team. Days after qualifying for the NAIA national tournament in Kansas City by winning the Golden State Athletic Conference (GSAC) tournament, the 2020 national tournament was canceled.

There is no comparison to the many sacrifices that healthcare workers and community frontline workers make every day just to do their jobs. But to a college athlete, being denied the opportunity to compete in an end-of-the-season tournament was a huge disappointment.

"Looking back, that was such an emotional time for us," Xander Bowers remembered. "We were coming off this big run with the Golden State Athletic Conference (GSAC) tournament championship and an automatic bid to Kansas City. A few days later, it was all canceled. There was no closure to the season."

After six months of living with, and learning more about, the threat of COVID, many businesses and universities were just beginning to take the necessary steps to navigate and modify life while taking precautions to keep people safe. However, most of the fall sports seasons were either canceled or moved to the spring of 2021.

In September of 2020, Coach Jeff Rutter, head coach of the ACU Men's Basketball team, was on the phone or attending zoom meetings every day with other coaches, athletic directors, or the NAIA, discussing how the upcoming season would look for basketball. Many teams were canceling the entire season, some were limiting games, others were limiting travel. It was an uncertain time.

There is no comparison between trying to make a hospital or clinic safe for all and trying to schedule enough games to have a basketball season. Coach Rutter stated during the fall planning period, "I have been coaching college basketball for over twenty years, and this is, by far, the hardest I have had to work. There were so many calls to make and procedures to follow. Mandates and recommendations were different from state to state."

In case one has forgotten, here are some of the changes that affected the 2020–2021 basketball season. Testing, testing, and more testing was being done every day, with temperature and symptoms checks and testing before games and travel. No one can forget the uncomfortable procedure of having a cotton-tipped stick rammed up one's nostril to test for COVID, a sure guarantee to make the eyes water, cause one to wince in pain, and, possibly, make one sneeze.

Drive-through testing sites were found in unusual places such as stadium parking lots, shopping malls, fairgrounds, and colleges. The San Diego Padres and Seattle Mariners spring training facility in nearby Peoria, Arizona, was a popular place to test the ACU team members.

Megan Vetter, the basketball trainer at ACU, explained, "We were required to do more routine cleaning, limited contact, limit number of athletes in the clinic, masks, temperature checks, daily symptom checks, follow-up on individuals with symptoms, coordinate testing, contact-tracing, proper return to play, reports to the conference and NAIA, and much more. We still needed to continue with all normal duties as an athletic trainer. My goal and purpose was to ensure that my student-athletes were able to do what they love but to be able to do it safely." Megan also stated that, unfortunately, the training staff was also viewed as "the bad guys."

Do you remember attending a college basketball game during the 2020–2021 season? Probably not, because most facilities did not allow any fans, or just a small number of guests that were on a pass list. "It was difficult not to have many fans at games," commented Key Williams. "I am a player that feeds off energy and loves to play in front of a large crowd." Those who were able to attend the games were required to sit only by their family members and wear masks.

The players needed to wear masks on the bench, but not when they were playing on the court. The players and coaches on the sidelines sat on chairs that were six feet apart. There was also no hand-shaking line after the games. That was replaced by a friendly wave to the other team's bench and players as both teams exited the floor.

Despite all the trials and tribulations of COVID that season, ACU was able to finish the season at 10–0 in the GSAC and 24–2 overall. The men's team was able to compete in all the games that were on the schedule. Some had to be rescheduled, and the GSAC was split into two divisions. In order to limit the spread of the disease, the games were scheduled on back-to-back nights against the same opponent in the same location. It wasn't ideal, but it worked, and teams were grateful to be able to play basketball. Thankfully, the end-of-the-season tournaments were held in a modified format. March Madness was back on for 2021!

CHAPTER 2

MARCH SADNESS

"'For my thoughts are not your thoughts, neither are your ways my ways,' declares the Lord" (Isaiah 55:8–9).

NAIA Opening Round Weekend
Saturday, March 13, 2021
Activity Center, Lewis-Clark State College
Lewiston, Idaho
Carroll College Fighting Saints
Helena, Montana

Swish! Brendan Temple makes the second of two free throws for Carroll College of Helena, Montana, to lift the Saints to a 61–49 lead with 11:46 to play in the game.

Was this the way the 2020–2021 COVID basketball season would end for the fifth-ranked, 24–2 Arizona Christian University Firestorm basketball team? A double-digit loss! "Trailing by a huge margin to a great team was new territory for us," Robby Wilson recalled. "Normally, we were in control of almost all of our games this season."

Unranked Carroll, with a 17–7 record, had won the previous night over Texas Wesleyan in the opening round of the NAIA forty-eight-team national tournament. ACU received a first-round bye, and had not played a game since the regular season finale on February 27, fourteen days earlier. "Some of our practices leading up to this game were not as crisp and sharp as I thought they should be," Coach Rutter admitted. There was no Golden State Athletic Conference tournament because of COVID. That was the reason for the long layoff between games.

The answer was "No," the season would not end in a blowout loss in the NAIA tournament on March 13, 2021. The Firestorm was able to respond with an 11–0 scoring run in the next three minutes of play. It was capped off with a three-point basket by ACU's Honorable Mention All-American point guard, Angelo Johnson (AJ), and two free throws by ACU's big man, Robby Wilson.

There was now 8:34 left to determine which team would advance to Kansas City (KC) for the Sweet 16, while the other team would see its season come to an end. Carroll's lead was cut to one point to 61–60, and the momentum was clearly with the Firestorm.

The scoring run was stopped when Jovan Šljivančanin of Carroll scored an offensive rebound. Gui Pedra scored on the next trip down the court for the Saints, and the lead was back to five points, 65–60, with 7:21 left to play.

ACU's Darius Goudeau hit a three-point basket from the right corner off of a baseline pass from AJ to cut the lead to two.

While his teammate, Bryce Davis, scored on the next possession with a six-foot, right-handed hook shot in the lane to tie the score at 65 with just under six minutes left. This game had the feel of a classic in the making.

Carroll's Jonny Hillman and the Firestorm's Goudeau both connected from long range to keep the teams even at 68, all with just over five minutes left to play.

The Saints regained a four-point advantage with free throws from Jovan and Shamrock Campbell's twelve-foot jumper in the lane. ACU was now down 72–68.

With five seconds left on the shot clock, AJ answered for ACU with a deep three-pointer from the left wing to cut the lead to one, 72–71 with just under four minutes left.

Carroll's Jovan connected twice from the line, and then he scored on a left-hand drive to put the Saints up five with 2:27 left to play. The score was now 76–71.

Goudeau continued his hot shooting, and he completed a four-point play, hitting a long-range jumper from the top of the key and drawing a foul. Darius hit the free throw to cut the lead to one at 76–75 with 2:09 left with a trip to KC, the site of the national finals on the line.

Ifeanyi Okeke dunked on a baseline cut and drop-off pass from Jovan to put the Saints up three.

While driving down the right base-line, Xander Bowers drew a foul for ACU and connected on both free throws 78–77 Carroll with :83 seconds left to the final horn. This was one of those games that makes the month of March such a won-derful time of the year for basketball fans, coaches, and players.

Jovan scored again after driving right and spinning back to shoot a left-handed hook in the lane for Carroll 80–77. Coach Jeff Rutter used a time-out with :57 left on the clock. There was not any panic during the time-out. All eyes were on the drawing board as Coach Rutter calmly and carefully drew up the play that the team was going to run, coming out of the time-out. It was a play they had regularly practiced throughout the season.

After getting the ball inbounds, Xander Bowers cut off a backscreen set by Darius. AJ found Xander open under the basket for a slam dunk. That pulled the Firestorm to within one point with :47 left, 80–79. Carroll used a time-out.

With :22 left to play, Campbell drove from the left wing to pull up for a tough thirteen-foot jumper in the lane over solid defense. This was Campbell's eleventh basket out of twelve attempts from the field for the day to put the Saints in front, 82–79.

Coach Rutter used another time-out. During this time-out, one could feel tension in the huddle. These players had been in big moments in big games before. This was it! A three-pointer was needed to tie the score, and time was running out. Most likely, the game would be decided with this possession. Eyes were all focused on the drawing board as Coach Rutter reviewed and drew up the play the Firestorm planned to execute.

ACU ran an elevator screenplay to get the ball into the hands of the hot-shooting Goudeau, but the three-point attempt, this time, was short. The missed shot was rebounded by Okeke for Carroll. Quickly, Okeke was fouled by Bowers with five seconds left to stop the clock.

Okeke made the second of two free throws to make it a four-point game, 83–79, and iced the game for the Saints. AJ had a final three-point attempt from the top of the key, but he could not connect as time expired.

Carroll rejoiced in the victory, while the ACU team slowly and painfully made the long walk back to the locker room. As had been the case all year long, there was no hand-shake line, just a distant wave, like all the games during the COVID season.

The final statistics were as close as the score. Both teams shot over 50 percent from the field. Carroll was 14–18 from the charity stripe, while ACU was 11 for 11. Both teams had 26 rebounds. Turnovers for the game: 9 for the Saints and 13 for the Firestorm.

Shamrock Campbell led all scorers with 26 points, 11 of 12 FG 92 percent.

Jovan Šljivančcanin, 18 points and 8 rebounds.

Ifeanyi Okeke, 13 points and 4 boards.

ACU had five players with double figures:

Goudeau, 21 points, 6 three-pointers, and 6 rebounds.

Johnson, 17 points, 5 three-pointers.

DeRon Kyle, 12 points, 5 rebounds.

Xander Bowers, 12 points, 4–4 FG, and 4–4 FT.

Bryce Davis, 10 points in nineteen minutes of play.

It was a solemn ACU locker room after such a hard-fought game. It is never easy to see a season come to an end. Since this was the final game of the season, several players and coaches shared some thank-yous and thoughts on this unusual year. Coach Rutter closed our team by gathering us all together in prayer.

The Firestorm played well enough to win, but Carroll was just a little better on this Saturday afternoon. This difficult defeat became a motivational springboard for the next season.

"We had a few mistakes that hurt us, but we learned what it takes to win at this tournament level," AJ shared later.

Bryce Davis reflected back on that setback in 2021. "That game gave us a ton of motivation that, I think, led into our big run this season."

"This is not the way the season was supposed to end," ACU senior Travis Walker stated after the game. "This ACU team accomplished so much during an unpredictable COVID basketball season."

The Firestorm finished 10 and 0 in the GSAC, and finished 24–3 on the season. Because of COVID, many players received another year of eligibility to compete again in 2021–2022. Besides Walker, one of the other players who would not return in 2021–2022 would be DeRon Kyle. Kyle made the All-Conference GSAC team and NAIA All-American team, great accomplishments under trying circumstances.

CHAPTER 3

MEET THE
2021–2022 TEAM

"'For I know the plans I have for you,' declares the Lord, 'plans to prosper you and not to harm you, plans to give you hope and a future'" (Jeremiah 29:11).

"A man's heart plans his course, but the Lord directs his steps" (Proverbs 16:9).

There is an old saying: "You can't win the Kentucky Derby with a donkey." The same can be said for any solid team. There must be some thoroughbreds on your roster. This ACU team was filled with a combination of thoroughbreds and workhorses. This is the road the players traveled before arriving at ACU.

#0 Chris Daniels, 6'3," Senior, Palmdale, California

Chris played one year at Glendale Community College (California). He was named All-Conference, averaging 15 points, 5 rebounds, and 4 assists per game. Chris also played one season at Fresno City College to help the Rams advance to the state semifinals.

Chris played varsity for two years at Highland High School, where the Bulldogs won the Golden League Championship. Daniels made the All-Golden League team. He averaged 13 points and 5 assists per game.

Chris's major is business with an emphasis in marketing. He would like to own a business someday.

From Coach Rutter: "Chris is versatile on offense and defense. He can play multiple positions, and he is long and athletic."

#1 Angelo Johnson, 5'8," Junior, Melbourne, Florida

AJ played two years at College of Central Florida. He was named All-Mid-Florida Conference. Johnson averaged 11 points, 6 assists, and 3.5 rebounds per game.

Florida Prep Academy is where AJ played two seasons, and his team advanced to the state championship game. AJ made the All-State team.

AJ is majoring in business, and he desires to play professional basketball.

From Coach Rutter: "Impactful, he makes other players better. AJ is an extremely hard-working, gifted guard."

#2 Dominic Gonzalez, 6'3," Freshman, Glendale, Arizona

Dom was a four-year varsity player for Ironwood High School. He helped the Eagles win the 5A Arizona State Championship and advanced to the state playoffs every year. Gonzalez was named First Team All-State, Region Player of the Year, and two-time District Player of the Year. He finished as the IHS leader in points, assists, and made three-pointers. His senior year, Dom averaged 19 points, 6 rebounds, and 2 steals per game.

Dom selected ACU because of the strong basketball and education programs, the coaches, and the enthusiasm and welcome he experienced.

Business administration is Dom's major. He hopes to play basketball professionally.

From Coach Rutter: "Dom is a smart and mature player. He is a good shooter and played on a winning program in high school."

#3 Micah Bradford, 6'0," Post-Grad, Bourbonnais, Illinois

Micah was a four-year varsity player at Bradley-Bourbonnais High School. He averaged 19 points a game as a senior and was a two-time All-Conference selection. He finished his career as all-time leading scorer.

Bradford was at Valparaiso University in Valparaiso, Indiana, for three seasons. Bradford averaged 5 points per game in his first two seasons. Injuries sidelined him for his third season. Micah earned a communication degree during that time.

Micah transferred to Southern University in Baton Rouge, Louisiana, for the 2019–2020 season, where he averaged 9 points per game.

From Coach Rutter: "Micah had Division 1 experience and has scoring skills. He also became a solid defender for us."

#4 Dennis Flowers, 6'3," Sophomore, Chicago, Illinois

Dennis played two seasons at Carroll College in Montana. He helped the Saints advance to the quarterfinals of the NAIA

National Tournament in 2021. Dennis made All-Frontier Conference Honorable Mention. Dennis averaged 10 points a game.

St. Francis High School is where Dennis played for four years. He helped the Knights reach the California Interscholastic Federation CIF quarterfinals. Twice, he was named as First Team All-Mission League. His senior year, he averaged 17.5 points, 6 rebounds, 4 assists, two steals per game. Dennis also ran track.

Dennis is a communications major and would like to become a sports analyst after playing professional basketball. Flowers chose ACU in order to grow in his faith and strengthen his athletic ability. Psalm 91 is his favorite chapter of the Bible. Dennis is also a talented pianist.

From Coach Rutter: Dennis was a double-digit scorer at a solid NAIA program. He can make tough shots, and he is a solid on-ball defender."

#5 Marcus Green, 6'4," Freshman, Pasadena, California

Marcus was a three-year varsity player at Etiwanda High School. He helped the Eagles win a state championship and two Baseline League championships. Marcus was named First Team All-State, First Team All-Baseline League, and Second Team All-CIF. He averaged 19 points, 7 rebounds, and 3 assists his senior year.

ACU was Marcus's college choice because of the coaching staff and the chance to grow in his faith. Marcus's dad played football at

Portland State, and his mom owns a USC track and field athletic championship record. His major is communication, and he looks forward to a career in journalism.

From Coach Rutter: "Marcus has rare power and jumping ability. He comes from a successful high school program."

#10 KeyVaughn Williams, 6'2," Junior, Glendale, Arizona

KeyVaughn (Key) Williams played high school basketball at nearby Deer Valley High School in Glendale. Bryce Davis was his teammate, and Key was a starter on the state 5A runner-up and finished the year at 26–3. Key averaged 15 points, 7 boards, 3 assists, and 3 steals his senior season. He was awarded All-Region 2nd Team and Defensive Player of the Year.

Coach Josh Cole coached at Deer Valley and helped Williams earn a scholarship to play for the Firestorm. Coach Cole later joined the ACU staff, making it very appealing for Key to attend ACU. Williams added, "It was also a school where I was able to grow in my faith and learn more about God."

His major is secondary education.

Key is a coach on the court. He has a photographic memory when it comes to running offensive sets and knows all of the opponents' plays. His basketball IQ allows him to be disruptive on the defensive end. Williams also is that player on the team with the quick wit and one-liners.

From Coach Rutter: "KeyVaughn has a competitive, feisty attitude. He also can defend many positions, and he is a crafty passer."

#11 Patrick Fisher, 6'0," Junior, Bloomington, Illinois

Pat played one season at Gavilan college and helped the Rams win a Coast Conference South Championship. He was named Coast Conference South Honorable Mention. He averaged 8 points, 5 assists, and 4 rebounds.

At Bloomington High School, Pat played three years and helped lead the Raiders to a third-place finish at state. He was named First Team All-Big Twelve and Second Team All-State.

Pat's major is business administration, and he would like to be a CEO of his own company in the future. He enjoys music and writing his own music.

From Coach Rutter: "Pat is an old-school, tough point guard. He has great instincts and can score when needed."

#14 Paul Hayden, 6'4," Freshman, Phoenix, Arizona

Paul played three years as a varsity player at Sunnyslope High School in Phoenix. His team actually lost to Ironwood High School (ACU's Dominic Gonzalez's team) in the state semifinals his senior year. He also played one year of varsity football.

His major is in business, and he plans to go into the ministry after graduation.

Paul was recruited by Coach Josh Cole. Paul played for Coach Cole's AAU team, and Coach Cole helped lead Paul to become a Christian in his sophomore year of high school. Paul decided on attending ACU after prayer and sensing the Lord's direction and provision giving him the opportunity to play basketball at ACU. Paul added, "The basketball program and the coaches were a big factor in my decision. Also, the Christian faith aspect that is taught in classes was an attraction. The coaches were legit followers of Christ, and it showed."

From Coach Rutter: "We saw Paul play as a sophomore for a successful high school program. He has a great shooting range, and Paul's character is a good fit for ACU."

#15 Xander Bowers, 6'7," Senior, Gilroy, California

Xander played two years at Gavilan College and helped the Rams go undefeated in conference. He was First Team All-State and averaged 12 points, 10 rebounds, 3 blocks, and 2 steals, shooting 70 percent from the floor.

He was a three-year varsity player at Christopher High School, where he averaged 18 points, 12 rebounds, 2 blocks, and 2 steals per game. Xander also played three years of varsity football and two seasons of lacrosse.

His major is business, and his goal is to own and operate an animal shelter.

From Coach Rutter: "Xander came from a 27–3 team in junior college. He is a game-changer with his superior athletic ability on both ends of the floor."

#21 Darius Goudeau, 6'5," Senior, Mesa, Arizona

He played one season at Cal State San Marcos, where he averaged 6 points and 4 rebounds. Darius also played two seasons at Phoenix College. He earned First Team All-Region and Second Team All-ACCAC. He led the Bears with 20 points and 9 rebounds as a sophomore.

Darius was a four-year varsity player at Mesa High School. He helped the Jackrabbits win a state championship. He was a two-time second-team All-State selection. He also played volleyball and finished as state runner-up one season.

Proverbs 3:5 is his favorite verse. He chose ACU to grow as a person mentally and spiritually and to develop strong relationships.

His major is business, and he is looking forward to owning several businesses.

From Coach Rutter: "Excellent shooter and rebounder. Darius plays tough and has great character."

#23 Xavier Cooper, 6'2," Junior, Denver, Colorado

Xavier played two seasons at Allan Hancock. He was named First Team All-Western State Conference North Division. He averaged 8 points, 7 rebounds, and 3 assists per game.

George Washington High School is where Xavier played for four years. He helped the Patriots win two 5A Denver Prep League Championships. Twice, he was named First Team All-Denver Prep League. Xavier also participated in track and field.

His favorite verse is John 3:16. His major is business administration. He would like to own a business in the future.

From Coach Rutter: "Xavier is a special defender because of his strength. He is a hard-nosed player.

#24 Bryce Davis, 6'7," Junior, Glendale, Arizona

Bryce Davis (BD) played for two seasons at the University of Incarnate Word in Texas. He appeared in thirty-three games and scored 14 points versus St. Francis (Illinois).

He was a four-year varsity player at Deer Valley High School in Glendale. ACU's KeyVaughn Williams was a teammate on the Deer Valley state finals team in 2018. He was named First Team All-Region and Regional Player of the Year. Davis averaged 19 points and 9 rebounds his senior year.

Bryce was recruited by ACU in high school, but Davis signed with D1 Incarnate Word in Texas instead. Bryce transferred to ACU in the fall of 2020, and he was able to play in the spring semester of 2021. Bryce also played for Coach Cole in a summer league and developed a strong relationship with him. Bryce decided to transfer to ACU because it was closer to home, he could grow in his faith, and ACU has a solid basketball program. BD is a big guy with a long wing-span, and he "plays tough" on the floor. Off the floor, he is a soft-spoken, kind young man. Bryce's grandmother passed away during the season, and it was a really tough time for Bryce and his family. Both of his parents played college basketball, Dad at Kansas State and Mom at Allen County (KS).

His favorite verse is 1 Corinthians 13:4. His major is business, and he hopes to play basketball beyond college.

From Coach Rutter: "Bryce is a great fit for our university. He is coachable, has good footwork, and is a tremendous scorer in the post."

#32 Robby Wilson, 6'9," Senior, Tucson, Arizona

Robby played two seasons at Pima Community College in Tucson. He helped the Aztecs finish as the national runner-up and won two ACCAC championships. Wilson was named First Team All-Conference and averaged a double-double as a sophomore.

Salpointe Catholic High School is where Robby played for four years. He helped the Lancers win a state championship, and he was named All-League.

Robby is majoring in secondary education, and he also plans to coach basketball.

From Coach Rutter: "Robby had many offers coming out of junior college. He is not the most athletic player, but his work ethic, character, and personality make him special."

#42 Shaun Wahlstrom, 6'8," Junior, Goodyear, Arizona

Shaun played at Estrella Foothills High School. He helped the Wolves advance to the state playoffs. He averaged 12 points and 9 rebounds and earned First Team All 4A Conference. Shaun played football for one year and did four years of track and field. He qualified for the state finals all four years in discus and javelin.

Wahlstrom played club basketball with Coach Cole. Cole then came on staff at ACU and recruited Wahlstrom to ACU. Shaun was attracted to the Firestorm because of Coach Cole and the opportunity to grow in his Christian faith. His favorite verse is 1 Timothy 4:12. His major is secondary education and business. He wants to flip houses.

Wahlstrom also participates in track and field for ACU. Shaun has several school records with the discus and javelin events. He helped the Firestorm win their first GSAC Track and Field Championship.

From Coach Rutter: "Shaun comes from a successful high school program. He is strong, competes, and rebounds well. Another player with solid character for our program."

Managers:

Avery Alday played baseball and basketball at Desert Christian High School in
Tucson. This is Alday's second season with
helping the Men's Basketball program.

Andrew Yarger was a classmate of
Avery's at Desert Christian. He also played
basketball and baseball for the Eagles.
Besides working for the Men's Basketball
program, Andrew also competes with one
of ACU's developmental teams.

Coaches:

Jeff Rutter

The 2021–2022 season marks the tenth season for Coach Rutter at Arizona Christian University. At the start of the season, Coach Rutter is two victories shy of two hundred career wins. Along with his coaching duties, Coach Rutter serves as the VP of Enrollment for ACU.

Prior to taking over at ACU, Coach Rutter spent ten years as an assistant coach at Azusa Pacific University and the previous two years as an assistant coach at California Baptist University.

Before coaching, Rutter played two years at Concordia University Irvine and two years at Cypress College. He earned All-Orange Empire League honors as a sophomore at Cypress after scoring 14 points a game on the strength of 79 made three-pointers.

Academically, Coach Rutter earned a bachelor's degree in organizational leadership from Biola University in 2005.

Hudson Welty

Coach Welty joined the ACU coaching staff in June of 2021. Coach Welty spent the previous two years as an assistant coach at Indiana Wesleyan University (IWU).

During his two seasons at IWU, the Wildcats produced a record of 59–7 and were ranked in the top three of the NAIA during that time, which includes the number-one ranking in the last five polls.

Prior to coaching at IWU, Coach Welty was an assistant for two years at Covenant College.

As a student-athlete, Welty graduated and played four years at MidAmerican Nazarene University in Kansas.

Caleb Oetjen (C.O.)

Coach O. was added to the ACU coaching staff before the start of the 2021–2022 season.

The last two seasons, Coach O. was on the coaching staff at Mount Vernon Nazarene University in Ohio.

Prior to coaching, Coach O. played professionally overseas in Lithuania and Germany.

Collegiately, C.O. spent four years at Bethel University (Indiana). Bethel was ranked nationally in every poll while Oetjen was playing at Bethel. He finished with just over 1,200 points and capped off his career as an NAIA First Team All-American.

Jackson Oldham (J.O.)

Coach J.O. is entering his second season at ACU. Coach Oldham helps with the prospect club teams, along with recruiting, player development, and scouting.

The winning program at ACU and the positive communication between players and coaches during open gyms attracted Oldham to ACU. Jackson desired to be under the leadership and influence of strong Christian men.

Prior to ACU, Coach J.O. assisted NBA Player Development Coach Phil Beckner.

Oldham spent his collegiate career playing basketball and baseball at Friends University in Nebraska and Iowa Central Community College. Twice, he was named as a NAIA Scholar-Athlete Honors.

Coach J.O. graduated from Friends in 2020 with a degree in business administration.

Scott Mossman

Coach Mossman enters his first year as an assistant coach at ACU. Mossman has over twenty years of college basketball coaching experience a head coach and as an assistant coach.

Mossman has coached at Grand Canyon University, Biola University, and California Baptist. Mossman gave Coach Rutter his first coaching position, when he was the head coach at Cal Baptist.

When Mossman wasn't coaching, he remained involved with basketball. He helped start, and was a part-owner of, Synergy Sports Technology. Synergy provides highly detailed statistical and video-clip analysis for the NBA, college, and international teams.

Coach Mossman grew up in the Phoenix area and played high school basketball at Sunnyslope. After two seasons at Scottsdale Community College, he attended MidAmerican Nazarene College in Kansas. There, he graduated with a degree in physical education.

Jack Vande Zande (Coach V.)

Coach V. begins his second season at ACU. Prior to ACU, Coach V. coached college and high school basketball and taught middle school English in Wisconsin for over twenty years. As an assistant coach, he helped Edgewood College of Madison, Wisconsin advance to the NAIA Division II National Tournament. Vande Zande made coaching stops at Pardeeville High School, West Bend West High School, and West Bend East High School (the last fifteen years before ACU).

ACU gave Coach V. the opportunity to assist with a college basketball program and be involved with sports ministry.

Much of this squad was recruited by two former assistant coaches who left ACU after the 2020–2021 season to pursue other career opportunities. Even though they were not at practices or on the sidelines during games, these coaches continued to stay in contact with the players throughout the season. If their schedules permitted, they would attend ACU home games to support the guys.

Trey Clarkson was assistant coach for ACU for four years and was responsible for recruiting some of the players who make up this team. Clarkson left coaching after the 2021 season to pursue a career with the family business—sort of. He is a third-generation State Farm agent in Arizona.

"The main thing I was looking for when recruiting to ACU was finding young men that cared. Particularly, guys that cared about winning and communicated they wanted to grow in their Christian faith. Both Robby and AJ fit those two categories. Whenever you find talented players that care, you will have a good team. Nowadays, it is difficult to find players that care more about the team than their own personal accolades.

"When one cares about winning, you will: (1) Work hard to improve, and (2) Accept your role and do it to the best of your ability.

"Robby Wilson has never been the most talented player in any gym, but because he wants to win so badly, he willed his way to two straight All-Conference selections. That definitely exceeded what I thought he would achieve.

"It is easy to find talent! It is hard to find TSU plus talent. AJ, Dennis, Robby, Xander, Bryce, Darius, Dom, and Paul all embody TSU plus talent.

"Finally, I also must acknowledge Callum Lawson, who really helped ACU turn the corner. Lawson is one of the best players at ACU, and he is enjoying a successful professional basketball career in Europe."

Josh Cole was an assistant coach for ACU for five years. After the 2021 season, Coach Cole accepted a math-teaching position and became the boys' varsity head basketball coach at O'Connor High School in the Phoenix area.

"Xander Bowers is an elite athlete. We learned about him during his freshman season at Gavilan Junior College in California. Coach Dallas Jenson sent us a highlight tape on Xander, and we knew it was a guy we were going to pursue hard. Xander's ability to defend multiple positions is what really stuck out, and we also found out, later, that Xander has a high basketball IQ."

KeyVaughn Williams was coached by Coach Cole when he was in sixth grade. Coach Cole also coached Key when he was a freshman and sophomore at Deer Valley.

Coach Cole added, "Key was recruited by several junior colleges, but he reached out to me about ACU. Coach Rutter went to watch him play, and he liked the edge that

KeyVaughn played with. Key has a high basketball IQ and is special on defense."

Bryce Davis was a teammate of KeyVaughn's at Deer Valley High School. He also was coached by Coach Cole in high school. Coach Cole added this: "Bryce is a special talent, and he moves real well for his size. We pursued Bryce after high school, but he was getting some D1 interest. He ended up going to Incarnate Word in San Antonio for two seasons. After battling some injuries, he decided to transfer. Coach Rutter and I got on him, and we were able to get him to come to ACU. He is a great fit for our program."

Paul Hayden went to Sunnyslope High School, where he competed in a couple of state championships and a couple of final fours. Coach Cole observed, "We knew from a faith standpoint that Paul was a great fit; he also was a player that would fit our system. Coach Rutter and I went to watch Key and Bryce play against Paul's team in the state championship when Paul was a sophomore.

Coach Rutter told Paul's mom that he was looking forward to coaching Paul in college." Thankfully, Paul decided to attend ACU, and Coach Rutter is now coaching him.

Dominic Gonzalez was a player we were on even before he was at Ironwood High School, just down the road from the ACU campus. Coach Cole added, "Coach Rutter and I would attend some of Dom's high school practices. Dom had a lot of people in his ear telling him that NAIA wasn't a good enough level for him. The relationship Coach Rutter and I had built with Gonzalez was the key. Dom knew that we had his best interest in mind, well beyond basketball.

CHAPTER 4

A FRESH START

"Therefore, encourage one another and build each other up, just as, in fact, you are doing. May the God who gives endurance and encouragement give you the same attitude of mind toward each other that Christ Jesus had" (1 Thessalonians 5:11).

Team Retreat, Labor Day Weekend

Classes for the fall semester at ACU began in August this year, so our team weekend retreat was held after two weeks of classes. Temperatures in September in the Phoenix area still get scorching hot, so

Coach Rutter planned the retreat at a higher elevation with cooler temperatures. This allowed the team to do some team-building activities outside.

On Friday morning, September 3, the team departed for Sedona, Arizona, to do some hiking with the wonderful scenery in God's creation. Sedona is known as a must-see area with its red-colored rock, green trees, and many hiking trails and shops.

It was amazing to find out that some players had never been on long hikes before. The Devil's Bridge hike allowed our players and coaches to walk alongside each other to become better acquainted. It was especially beneficial for the first-year assistant coaches in the program, Coach Hudson Welty and Coach Caleb Oetjen, to gain important insights into the players, plus share their personal goals and visions for the team during the four-mile hike.

"It was a rough beginning to the season," Xander Bowers recalled. "In the past two seasons, I had grown real close with Coach

Cole and Coach Clarkson, and now they are gone. It took a while for me to build up a solid relationship with our new staff members, Coach O. and Coach Welty."

After getting some lunch in Sedona, the team headed to Slide Rock Park. The first challenges of the weekend occurred at Slide Rock. A shallow river runs through the park, allowing individuals to slide through the water on long, flat rocks. Lots of fun! However, that was mild compared to the cliff-jumping that followed. The river drained into a lagoon that was surrounded by several different-sized cliffs to jump from. Many players and a few coaches jumped off of the thirty-foot cliff, and the bravest challenged themselves and plunged into the lagoon from a sixty-foot cliff!

"Jumping off the cliff is something I will always remember. It forced many players to do something uncomfortable and unforgettable," Senior Robby Wilson proclaimed. Some players were one and done, while others made several jumps off the cliff.

"Without the encouragement from my teammates and coaches, I never would have jumped off the cliff," Paul Hayden added.

When late afternoon rolled around, we loaded up the vans to drive over to Prescott, Arizona. We were going to spend the rest of our time together at Prescott Pines. During our evening team time, Coach Rutter divided the players into small groups in order to brainstorm ideas for standards that both the coaches and team could agree upon. The standards had to tie in to one of the three pillars for ACU Basketball, which are: *Tough, Smart, and Unselfish*. With the players' input, the coaches settled on these Seven Standards for ACU Basketball 2021–2022 season.

1. No BCD (Blame, Complain, or Defend)
2. TSU Time (Show up ten minutes before a team event is to start)
3. Calling Up (Making teammates accountable for standards)

4. Extra Mile (Do more than what is expected)
5. Celebrate Your Teammates
6. Know Your Scout
7. Four Hands/Huddle (Team Huddle on floor)

"It was a great idea for the coaches to allow the players to come up with the team standards," Robby Wilson shared. "It gave the team ownership of how certain things of the basketball program should operate. It empowered the players to call out and keep players accountable."

"This was unique for me," Dennis Flowers III added. "I have never been a part of building a culture map for a team from the ground level."

On Saturday morning, after breakfast, Coach Chambers challenged the team members to keep growing in their faith. The message he shared was based on the team scripture for the ACU basketball season from 1 Corinthians 16:13–14: "Be watchful, stand firm in the faith, *act like men,* be strong. Let all that you do be done in love" (ESV).

More challenges were awaiting the players and coaches after lunch.

"WHOOOOAAAAA!" senior Chris Daniels yelled as he jumped off the platform and started his ride down the cable of the zipline. Daniels recalled later, "The events of the retreat helped me overcome my fear of heights." All the players and most of the coaches took part in finishing the two zipline runs. For many, this was the first time to experience the thrill of a zipline ride. A bigger challenge was still ahead.

After a short walk on this beautiful afternoon through the woods, the team was led to the Ropes Course area. There were several events planned to give the players an opportunity to take a risk. Course number one challenged the players to climb up a tree twenty-five feet, stand on a small platform— and then jump, grab a trapeze bar, and swing! If a player missed the bar or slipped off the bar after grabbing it, the safety rope would catch the individual. The second course was the biggest challenge of the day. Each team member was expected to climb twenty-five feet up the tree, then walk across wooden planks that were spaced ten inches apart, which were suspended on cables between two trees. The trees were twenty feet apart. Upon reaching the second tree, the player needed to jump off the platform and then slowly be lowered to the ground by the safety rope that was connected to him. Some players did not even consider either one of the courses; some were encouraged by their teammates to give it a try. Others tried both of the ropes courses.

After dinner, the team met again for a brief, but entertaining, talent show put on by the incoming freshmen. That was followed by a spiritual workout with Coach Chambers as he challenged the team again with a short message based on our team scripture for the season. The evening wrapped up by gathering under the beautiful evening stars with a campfire and s'mores.

Sunday morning after breakfast, the team headed back to the ACU campus. The team had the rest of Sunday and Labor Day Monday to recover and finish school work. Classes would resume on Tuesday.

The season was off to a great start after the weekend retreat. "The retreat set the tone relationally for our team for the season," Assistant Coach Welty added. "Our guys got to spend quality time together, hiking, exploring, playing games, and hanging out during the course of the weekend. The team set standards in place and dove deeper into what God had in store for us for the season."

CHAPTER 5

WORK BEFORE PLAY

"Do you not know that in a race, all the runners run, but only one gets the prize? Run in such a way as to get the prize. Everyone who competes in the games goes into strict training. They do it to get a crown that will not last, but we do it to get a crown that will last forever" (1 Cor. 9:24–25).

With the fun and somewhat-relaxing retreat behind them, the players now had team weight-lifting workouts for the next three weeks on Monday and Wednesday mornings at 6:00 a.m. Dynamic Sports Training (DST) was hired by the school to train ACU's athletes. Coach Ray Karvis heads up the strength program for the Men's Basketball program. "Most basketball players don't love the weight room like football players," Coach Karvis noted. "I had to earn the players' trust, which takes time. I wanted to challenge them more this fall. They responded well and benefited greatly from their dedication."

Several of the Super 7 Standards kicked in right away for the first team weight-lifting session. The first standard TSU time meant the college students needed to be at the weight room by 5:50 a.m. Ah, that didn't happen the first Monday. Players learned responsibilities by calling teammates the night before and/or early in the morning to get everyone to the workout on time to avoid being assigned extra work.

"It is easy to work out in the afternoon," Coach Welty proclaimed. "The purpose behind the early morning workouts and junkyard workouts was to put our team to the test and do something difficult together.

It's hard to bring energy to lift your teammates up in the early morning hours
of the day."

On Friday mornings, instead of weights,
a junkyard workout was held on one of the
new turf fields on campus. This was a type
of physical and mental workout that Coach
Welty and Coach Oetjen brought into the
program. The best way to describe a junkyard workout is a land-only version of
what the US Navy Seals go through in their
training regimen. Coach Welty came up with
eight different stations that the players had
to rotate through in order to work different
muscle groups. Some of the stations included
pushing a weighted sled eighty yards, whip-
ping heavy ropes, tossing a sixteen-pound
medicine ball along with burpees, push-ups
with weight plates on their backs, abdomen
crunches/planks, and the bear crawl. The
overtime period of this workout included
players running six 100-yard dashes.

"These workouts really made us mentally stronger," Flowers III noted. "Plus it

allows players to look at physical pain in a different way."

"Junkyards took me back to some of the conditioning workouts we had in high school football," Shaun Wahlstrom added later. "It was so taxing, physically and mentally."

Before the junkyard workouts started, while it was just starting to get light outside, Coach Welty shared Proverbs 11:25 with the team: "A generous person will prosper, whoever refreshes others will be refreshed." Coach used this scripture to remind the players to encourage each other as they made their way through the grueling exercises. "This verse will help take the focus off of your pain and misery, and think of others instead."

Later, Chris Daniels agreed with that statement, "By motivating others, it made it easier on myself."

At the beginning of each workout, Coach Welty called out a player's name, and that player selected another player as his workout partner to go through each station. Before the guys headed out to do the stations, each member of the team did an arm/upper body workout, lifting a forty-five-pound weight plate with six different lifts. Coach Welty, Coach Oetjen, and Coach Oldham also joined in on the workout. Coach Rutter and Coach V. made sure players were doing the proper amount of reps, monitored the players, and encouraged the players as they strained to finish certain events.

The better-conditioned players were able to struggle through the stations. There were players who needed teammates to cheer them on to get through the reps, and others collapsed on the turf after finishing a station.

"The junkyard workouts were key for our team and how to pull for one another," Team captain Robby Wilson admitted. A few were working so hard that they needed to go off to the side of the field to throw up. Our guys were straining and pushing their bodies to the max. Meanwhile, in the northern morning sky, twelve hot air balloons and their passengers were peacefully getting started on their Friday morning adventures. What a stark contrast of a Friday morning in the Valley of the Sun: grueling pain versus peaceful pleasure.

On September 24, 2021, the last of three junkyards was held. The players were finished with their workout and thought they would be dismissed for the morning. Coach Welty had other plans. "Where was the energy, fellas? That was not a championship team effort! This is halftime. Get some water, and we need to go out and repeat the entire junkyard. You guys are better than that!" Coach Welty and Coach Oetjen joined the team to redo all of the stations on that early September morning.

"That was tough to go out and repeat that challenging workout again," AJ later recalled. "It was to make us or break us. There was a mental barrier that we needed to get over."

"At first, our guys were extremely hesitant to do the junkyard workouts," Coach Oetjen claimed later. "They warmed up to the concept of doing hard things together as a team."

After all the groups repeated the junk-yard, the team joined together to complete a two-minute abdominal plank. About thirty seconds into the plank, KeyVaughn Williams started singing, "Lean on Me when you're not strong . . ." One by one, team members joined in. "till I'm gonna need somebody to lean on." That was quite impressive! Inside, the coaches were smiling. This team has got it. They are coming together as a team after such a demanding workout to encourage each other through the words of a song. "That ended up being a theme of this team for the rest of the season," Robby Wilson stated later. "We knew when the game was not going well, we would lean on each other to turn things around."

CHAPTER 6

TIME TO GET AFTER IT

"Forget the former things; do not dwell on the past. See I am doing a new thing!"
(Isaiah 43:18).

Monday, September 27, 2022
The Events Center

"We pray this in Jesus's name." As we met at center court, Coach Rutter would have a player begin and end each practice with a prayer. This was the first official practice date for the 230 NAIA teams around the country. Expectations were running high on the first day of practice for the preseason seventh-ranked NAIA Firestorm team.

During the first week of practice, Coach Rutter reviewed many basic offensive and defensive principles. The first trial of the season occurred when several players tested positive for COVID, missing practice for several days. On October 4, there were only eleven players available to practice. Five players were out. Undaunted, Coach O. laced up the sneakers in order to have twelve players practicing that day.

By the middle of October, the players were returning from their COVID episodes, and several intrasquad scrimmages were held at the Events Center. Coach O. and Coach Welty would draft teams and coach them up. The team also had a scrimmage against Phoenix College on October 20.

Midnight Madness was held for the women's and men's teams on Monday, October 25. The teams were introduced to the fans gathered that evening. Darius Goudeau won the three-point shooting contest for the men, and Paul Hayden surprisingly won the slam dunk contest. "The only reason I won the slam dunk contest," Hayden humbly confessed, "is because I did not miss any of my dunks!" Opening night was just four days away.

October 29–30, 2021 Tim Fultz Memorial Classic at ACU

For several seasons, now, the Firestorm opened the season with the Fultz Classic. The Fultz Classic is named after Tim Fultz who was a student-athlete at Southwestern

College, now Arizona Christian University, preparing to be a missionary.

Tim was recruited to the 1985–1986 basketball team by Paul Westphal, former NBA player—not because of his basketball talent, but because he owned a car and could drive players to an off-campus practice site! His faith, work ethic, and commitment to the team was an inspiration. In the final seconds of a game that would send the team into the national playoffs, Tim sank two crucial free throws to win the game. Tim was carried off the court by his teammates.

Missionary work was Tim's calling. While a student, he went on several trips to build churches and share the message of Jesus Christ. In August of 1990, while in Africa, Tim was helping with construction of a church. In a tragic accident, Tim fell thirty-five feet from the roof to his death. Because of his willingness to donate several vital organs to local Africans, Tim's heart still beats in Africa today.

The Servant
Authored by a former teammate

He was not the most skilled or the best,
But he had worked hard
Under the watchful eye of his coach,
Under the watchful eye of his God,
Learning, practicing, training, waiting

To play
To serve.

The basketball game hung in the balance,
The souls of many hung in the balance.

Building upon on a winning record,
Building a house of worship,

And when the final shot fell,
And when he fell,

They carried him off, cheering;
They carried him off.

He played with his heart;
He gave his heart.

They called him a hero;
The Lord called him home.

O death, where is thy sting?
The strength of sin is the law,

But thanks be to God
Who giveth us the victory
Through our Lord
Jesus Christ.

"Therefore, my beloved brethren,
Be ye steadfast, unmovable
Always abounding in the Work of the Lord
Forasmuch as ye know that
Your labor is not in vain in the Lord."
1 Corinthians 15:55–56

Well done,
Good and faithful servant

In loving memory of Tim Fultz

October 29, 2021
The Events Center
Embry-Riddle Eagles
Prescott, Arizona

The Firestorm was geared up to play a real game, for a change. It was a long five weeks of weight training and practicing and playing against the same guys every afternoon. "As the players took the floor for the first time of the year," Coach Karvis observed, "a fan could see that the ACU players were stronger and had been training."

This would be Embry-Riddle's first game in twenty-two months. No basketball games were played during the COVID 2020–2021 season. The starting lineup for the first game was Angelo Johnson (AJ), Dennis Flowers III, Darius Goudeau, Robby Wilson, and

Bryce Davis (BD). It did not take long for the Firestorm to take control of the game with their hot shooting and stingy defense against an over-matched team. The half-time score was 63–27. ACU shot 10 for 17 (58.8%) from three-point range in the half while holding Embry-Riddle to 37 percent from the field.

With such a large lead, Coach Rutter was able to get all the players at least seven minutes of game time. The Firestorm kept shooting the ball well from the floor. The final score was 124 to 52. All but one player scored for ACU. Flowers led the way with 18 points, hitting 5 of 6 from long range. "It was fun getting up and down the floor, " Flowers III commented. "My teammates welcomed me to the team and had confidence in me." Paul Hayden added 14, Dominic Gonzalez scored 13 points in thirteen minutes. Pat Fisher chalked up 10 points. The team shot a blistering 54 percent from behind the arc and nineteen three-pointers in a game, which tied a school record: Trevor Weir led Embry-Riddle with 13.

After his 199th career win at ACU, Coach Rutter commented on the win: "Everybody played well for us. We wanted to apply pressure and not let them get in a rhythm offensively. I am also pleased with the thirty assists our team had. Defense wins the game, but the offense tells you by how much. Offensively, we were efficient tonight, and we executed well.

"We are looking forward to Saturday afternoon's match-up with Antelope Valley (currently on a twenty-three-game winning streak dating back to the previous year)," Coach Rutter added. "Their quickness and athleticism is impressive, and they play really hard."

October 30, 2021
The Events Center
Antelope Valley Pioneers (AVU)
Lancaster, California

In less than twenty-four hours, the Firestorm was back in action. The Pioneers from Antelope Valley was a long and athletic team that trapped and forced teams to play fast and turn the ball over. A layup by Angelo Johnson (AJ) and 5 points from Robby Wilson gave ACU an early 7–0 lead.

Antelope Valley did not score its first basket until 15:57 left in the half—a three-pointer from Levontay Ott to make the score 7–3. ACU was able to maintain a lead for the next six minutes until AVU went on a 10–0 run to tie the score at 21 with 6:47 to play before halftime.

The teams exchanged baskets the rest of the half, but ACU was either tied or held the lead. The score at halftime was 30–28. Neither team was able to score in the last 1:50 of the half. Both teams turned the ball over often. AVU had 15 miscues at the half, while ACU had 11 turnovers. Wilson had 10 points at the break, while AJ had 8.

The second half saw the teams battle evenly. The score was knotted at 41–all with 14:11 left to play. Jamal Johnson hit a three-pointer for the Pioneers with just under ten minutes to play to give Antelope Valley its first lead of the game, 46–45.

The Firestorm responded with an 11–1 run in the next two and a half minutes. Paul Hayden got the momentum back for ACU with a jumper and three-pointer. Darius Goudeau added a four-point play with a long-range bomb and a free throw, and AJ added a jumper. It was 56–47 ACU with 7:14 to the final horn. AJ hit a three-pointer with 4:47 left to give the Firestorm a double-digit lead, 59–48.

The Pioneers were able to cut the lead to eight with three and a half minutes left, but then ACU closed the game on an 11–2 run, which left the final score at 70–53. The Firestorm was now 2–0 on the season, and Coach Rutter earned his 200th career win at ACU.

"Antelope Valley made it difficult to get into an offensive rhythm this afternoon. We had some guys set up and hit some big shots for us that helped us open the game up a bit," Coach Rutter commented after the win. "I was pleased with how we defended and battled for stops."

Wilson and Johnson led ACU with 16 and 15 points respectively. Paul Hayden had 10 points coming off the bench, while Darius Goudeau had 9.

Jamal Johnson led the Eagles with 10 points, and three players had 8 points apiece for Antelope Valley.

November 2, 2021
Scott Activity Center
Southern Assemblies of God University
(SAGU) American Indian College Warriors
Phoenix, Arizona

Today marked the first road game of the season. It was a short twenty-minute drive to SAGU. Before the game tipped off, there was a chance that the game would not take place. Several of the SAGU players were upset that the head coach was fired over the weekend, and the players were willing to forfeit the game in protest.

Coach Rutter and the team did not exactly know what happened behind the scenes, but the officials for the game showed up. There would be a game played. In the locker room before we took the court for warm-ups, Coach Rutter prayed for our team and the SAGU players and the interim coach.

As the game tipped off at 7:00 p.m., the Firestorm wore their new road uniforms, which were red, trimmed in yellow. Xander Bowers did not suit up because of some back issues. It did not take long for the Firestorm to build a double-digit lead. Robby Wilson led the first half charge with 17 first-half points—most coming from blistering three-point shooting. Wilson was 5 of 6 from long range. The score at the half was 58–28 ACU with a comfortable advantage.

The Firestorm kept rolling through the second half, and all the players on the roster played at least eight minutes. The final score was 118 to 56. The stifling, quick defensive guards for ACU, AJ, Micah Bradford, Dennis Flowers, and Patrick Fisher, recorded 16 steals and 28 turnovers. Five players scored in double figures for ACU. Wilson led the way with 19. Davis had 14–8 of 9 from the line. He also had 7 rebounds. Bradford finished with 12 points and 8 steals and 4 assists. Freshman Marcus Green scored 12 points, while AJ had 11 points and 5 assists. Chris Daniels had 9 points, while Goudeau and Shawn Wahlstrom each had 8. Ryan Pate had 9 points for the SAGU Warriors.

The only struggle the Firestorm had on this night was shooting free throws: 18–32 (56.3%). From the floor, ACU shot 57 percent. After the game, the team met in the corner of the gym. Coach Rutter prayed for the team and gave the schedule for Wednesday.

November 5, 2021
The Events Center
Park University Buccaneers
Gilbert, Arizona

The Firestorm was back in action on Saturday with a game against Park University of Gilbert, Arizona. Xander Bowers would not be available for the game. Once again, the Firestorm got off to an early lead—going up 11–0 just three minutes into the game. ACU kept building on the lead with AJ and Darius Goudeau, both scoring 8 points in the half to lead the Firestorm to a 48 to 24 halftime score.

The second half saw a lot of fouls called as both teams shot 30 free throws for the game. ACU shot a blistering 87 percent from the line at 26 of 30, while Park was 17 of 30, 57 percent. For the second time this week, the Firestorm cruised to a 97–52 win. Bryce Davis led the ACU attack with 16 points, going 6 of 7 from the floor. Wilson, AJ, and Gonzalez all had 11, while Bradford had 10 and Goudeau had 8 points and 10 rebounds. Dante Aganmwonyi led the Buccaneers with 13, with Craig Mueller chipping in 11 points.

November 10, 2021
The Events Center
Benedictine University Redhawks
Mesa, Arizona

It did not take long for the Firestorm to jump out to an early 7–0 lead, a minute and forty-five seconds into the game. Baskets by Johnson, Wilson, and Flowers gave the

Firestorm a lead that it would not relinquish. Benedictine's Stevie James hit a three-pointer to pull the Redhawks within four points with 15:30 left in the half. That would be the closest the Redhawks would ever get to the lead. ACU's Patrick Fisher's three-pointer, with 7:42 before the half, gave the home team its first ten-point lead of the game. By halftime, the lead was twelve points, 39–27.

ACU did not shoot it well the first half, going 2 for 15, 13 percent, from three-point range. Seven players for the Firestorm scored in the first half with Bryce Davis with 9, and Robby Wilson had 8 points and 8 rebounds. Jay Small led all scorers with 11 points for the Redhawks.

In the second half, ACU was able to build on the lead. A tip-in by Robby Wilson, a layup by Paul Hayden, and a jumper by Patrick Fisher extended the lead to twenty-four at 70–46, with 6:25 left in the game. The Firestorm maintained a comfortable lead until the final horn. ACU moved its record to 5–0 with 80–64 over Benedictine University.

"We settled for some tough shots early on, and several turnovers in transition seemed to keep stealing our momentum," was ACU Coach Rutter's take on the game. "Our guys did a better job on the offensive glass in the second half and created some offense that way. AJ and Bryce were limited by early foul trouble, but were able to have some nice moments. Pat and Robby both had great second halves to carry the scoring load."

Robby Wilson finished with a double-double with 15 points and 11 rebounds. Pat Fisher led the Firestorm with 16 points on 7 of 11, shooting from the floor. Bryce had 12 points, and AJ added 10 points. The Redhawks' Jay Small led all players with 18 points.

Arizona Christian will be on the road for its next six games, beginning with an exhibition game in Los Angeles against Loyola Marymount.

November 13, 2021
Albert Gersten Pavilion
Loyola Marymount University
Lions (LMU)
Los Angeles, California

The Firestorm had rolled through its first five opponents on the schedule. That would not be the case on this Saturday afternoon. ACU was in Los Angeles to play an exhibition game against the Lions of Loyola Marymount. An exhibition game is not included on the win/loss record. "The beautiful campus, the large gym, and the fans made this one of best atmospheres to play in all year," recalled Bryce Davis. ACU bench strength increased with Xander Bowers being cleared to play. The athletic 6'7" senior would be a huge asset in guarding a much taller LMU team.

ACU got on the scoreboard first when AJ nailed a three-pointer thirty seconds into the game. That lead was short-lived as LMU went on a 19-to-6 run in the next nine minutes to take a 19-to-9 lead, with 10:38 left in the half.

With just under four minutes left until intermission and the Firestorm down 28–23, Patrick Fisher went on a 7–0 scoring spree for ACU. Fisher scored 7 points in thirty-nine seconds with a jumper, three-pointer, and 2 free throws. ACU regained the lead at 30–28 with just over three minutes until the break. The firestorm was able to hold on to the lead and went into the locker room at half, up 35–32.

The ACU locker room was pleased with how the team was able to battle back from a ten-point deficit with several ACU players in foul trouble in the first half. The Firestorm players had expectations of competing well against a talented Loyola Marymount team. Coach Rutter reminded the team to play solid defense and execute on offense.

After being plagued with foul trouble in the first half, Bryce Davis got the ACU offense rolling in the second half. The 6'7" man in the middle scored 6 straight points on a jumper, 2 free throws, and a layup. "I was really focused going into this game," Davis later commented. "My teammates were very supportive." Davis's scoring allowed the Firestorm to maintain a 41–38 advantage with seventeen minutes left in the game.

In the next ten minutes, ACU went on to outscore LMU, 17 to 11 to take a 58–49 lead on 2 free throws from Davis. Just when it looked like ACU might be able to pull the upset, LMU came roaring back. The Lions went on an 18–0 run, and they regained the lead 67–58, with 1:44 left to play. During the scoring drought, ACU had 11 straight empty possessions with 5 turnovers (ACU would have 22 TOs on that day).

The Firestorm was able to pull within five points two times down the stretch. LMU's Joe Quintana hot shooting guard iced the victory by going 6 for 6 at the free throw line to close out the game. The final score was 74–67.

LMU's Quintana led all scorers with 26 points, going 6 for 9 from long range. Eli

Scott had a big second half, scoring 14 and 18 for the game. From the free throw line, LMU was 20–29, while ACU went 12 for 12. Davis led the Firestorm with 20 points going 6 for 7 from the floor and 8 for 8 from the free throw line. "Even though the game didn't end how we had hoped," Davis admitted, "it was an amazing environment and competitive game." Pat Fisher played well coming off the bench, scoring 10 points and gathering 6 rebounds. Darius Goudeau and Dennis Flowers III both finished with 9 points each. Robby Wilson did not score, but he had 7 assists.

"We wanted to come play our game and compete to win," Coach Rutter stated after the exhibition loss. "I am proud of the way we competed, but the game really changed with Robby, Bryce, Xander, and AJ all getting in foul trouble. We did not execute down the stretch as well as we needed to. It was a great game for us to learn from as we prepare for early conference games."

After the game, the team showered, grabbed a bite to eat, and made the six-hour trip back to Glendale, Arizona. The vans got back on campus at 2:30 a.m. However, the night was not over for the four assistant coaches. We still needed to return the rental vans to the airport—another thirty-minute drive. The coaches then took a shuttle bus back to the airport. Next, the four assistants rode the Sky Tram to the East Economy parking lot. As the coaches walked under the star-filled sky to their own cars to drive home, the overtired coaches were giddy, and they joked about putting in an all-nighter. "My parents are getting up at this time in Indiana to get ready for early Sunday morning church," Coach O. joked. Most coaches got home at 4:30 Sunday morning. Coach Rutter, by the way, smartly stayed back in the LA area to scout Hope International, a team that ACU would play in five days.

CHAPTER 7

LET THE GOLDEN STATE ATHLETIC CONFERENCE (GSAC) GAMES BEGIN

"Rejoice always, pray without ceasing, give thanks in all circumstances" (1 Thessalonians 5:16–18).

November 18, 2021
Darling Pavilion
Hope International University Royals
Fullerton, California

In the week heading up to the game, Coach Rutter shared that ACU was now ranked #4 in the NAIA, moving up three places from the preseason poll. Coach Rutter also shared that several teams from the GSAC were ranked in the top twenty-five.

ACU was selected by the conference coaches as the preseason favorite. Its first game was not going to be easy. First of all, Hope was ranked and picked to finish in the top three in the conference. Second, ACU is 0–10, playing at Hope International. Finally, ACU traveled to Los Angeles last weekend and now back to play two games in three days. ACU entered the game at 5–0, while Hope was 4–1.

Robby Wilson and Bryce Davis scored on back-to-back possessions to give the visiting team a 4–2 lead. In the next eight minutes, Hope went on a 17–6 run to give the Royals a 19–10 lead. ACU continued to struggle to score in the first half. Hope took a 36–25 halftime lead. The ice-cold shooting Firestorm shot 15 percent from long range (3–19) and 23 percent from the floor.

Coach Rutter tried different lineups to find a combination of players to score some points. Two free throws by Xander Bowers, and a jumper by Bryce Davis cut the lead to 8 points, 53–45 with 8:36 left to play. It was one of those games when the defense did not play up to its standards and shot the ball poorly. The team struggled to get into an offensive rhythm. Hope won going away 73-57.

After the game, Coach Rutter said the team was not Tough, Smart, and Unselfish, but the complete opposite. "We were Soft, Stupid, and Selfish tonight!" Coach Rutter disgustingly addressed the team in the locker room. Even after being honest and stern with the team, Coach Rutter concluded our team time together with a prayer.

Hope had four players score in double figures. Jalani Horn came off the bench to score 14 points. Josh Powell-Davis, 6'6" and 300 pounds-plus, was tough to handle inside for the Firestorm, scoring 13 points and 5 rebounds. Charles Neal had 12, and Sebastian Castro finished with 10. The Royals shot 51 percent from the floor, while

ACU shot 26 percent from the floor. Robby Wilson had 13 points and 8 boards for ACU, while Bryce Davis had 11 and 7.

"This is a game I will forget, but I will remember how we responded to it," Wilson added, weeks after the game. "This loss changed the trajectory of our season. As a team, would we be mature and learn and accept the team standards, or would we be selfish players and go our own ways?"

November 19, 2021

With the strict COVID mandates in California, it was sometimes difficult to find places to eat inside, and it was also difficult to find gyms to practice in. Such was the case on this Friday morning. The team ended up shooting and having a light practice at an LA Fitness gym right next to our hotel in Anaheim Hills. Coach Rutter wanted the team to get some shots up to regain some confidence before traveling down to the San Diego area. At the LA Fitness gym, the coaches intentionally walked around the gym to talk to players one-on-one on various subjects.

After the slow drive down I-5, we checked into the Best Western on Shelter Island. The team ate wings and pizza at Oggi's. One of the benefits of playing our "away" conference games in Southern California is the proximity to the Pacific Ocean; one of the negative items is the California traffic.

November 20, 2021
Salvation Army, El Cajon, California
San Diego Christian University
Hawks (SDC)

The Firestorm was hoping to play better offensively against a much-improved San Diego Christian University team from the previous season. AJ nailed a three-pointer :45 into the game to give the visiting team a 3–2 lead. That would be the only lead the Firestorm would have the entire first half. SDC went on a 15-to-7 run to take a 17–7 lead with 10:15 left before halftime. The

Hawks were able to keep the lead throughout the rest of the first half. In the last two minutes before intermission, Davis, Bowers, and AJ were able to score baskets to cut the lead to 3 at the half, 30–27. ACU's cold California shooting woes continued, only shooting 21 percent from the field and from long range. At halftime, Coach Rutter encouraged the team to make the extra pass. Give up the good shot for a great shot!

In the second half, the Hawks were able to maintain a small lead for the first six minutes. ACU's Paul Hayden hit a game-tying three-pointer with 13:16 left in the game. This sparked a 12–0 scoring run for ACU. The score was knotted at 38–all. On its next possession, Patrick Fisher connected on 2 free throws to give the Firestorm a lead that it would not give up. Two three-pointers by Dom Gonzalez and one by Dennis Flowers III helped give the Firestorm some breathing room.

A layup and a free throw by Bryce Davis extended the margin to 11 with just under a minute to play and a 68–57 advantage. The Firestorm was able to escape with a 69–63 victory over a scrappy and determined San Diego Christian team.

The Firestorm poured in 42 second-half points and shot 50 percent in the second half. Flowers was the only ACU player with double digits with 12. AJ added 9 points and 5 assists. Bowers and Davis each had 9 points. Robby Wilson scored 4 points with 10 rebounds. Gonzalez, Hayden, and Micah Bradford all had 6 points to give good scoring off the bench for ACU. Kavonte Kinney of SDC led all scorers with 18 points. The team was back on campus by 11:45 p.m. on Saturday night, much earlier than the previous weekend.

CHAPTER 8

TRIP TO THE SUNSHINE STATE FOR THANKSGIVING

"Oh give thanks to the Lord, for He is good, His steadfast love endures forever" (Psalm 107:1).

The Firestorm basketball team had the day off on Sunday, but it was time to fly to Miami on Monday afternoon. The team headed to the Seahawk Thanksgiving Classic, hosted by Keiser University in West Palm Beach, Florida. ACU would face Keiser on Tuesday night and Florida Memorial on Wednesday night. At this point in the season, Xander Bowers was going to be red-shirted. Bowers reflected later, "It was hard not knowing if I was playing or redshirting. The in-between really started to get to me mentally."

November 23, 2021
Student Life Center,
West Palm Beach, Florida
Keiser University Seahawks

For the third game in a row, ACU struggled to get going offensively. Coach Rutter started senior Micah Bradford in place of Darius Goudeau to switch things up a little for ACU. Keiser broke out to an early 9–0 lead. ACU came up empty on its first 7 possessions, including 3 turnovers. Bryce Davis scored a free throw three and a half minutes into the game to get the Firestorm on the board. Keiser would lead 11–1 before the Firestorm would begin clawing its way into the game. Three-pointers by three different ACU players (AJ, Pat Fisher, and freshman

Marcus Green) would tie the score at 14 with 12:30 left in the half.

The teams battled back and forth the next few minutes. With five minutes left before half, Darius Goudeau nailed a three-pointer to put ACU up 26–24. Micah Bradford had 4 points and Dom Gonzalez scored 5 points, including a jumper at the buzzer for the Firestorm in the final four minutes of the half to give ACU a 37–30 advantage at the break.

ACU came out red-hot to start the second half. AJ hit two three-pointers in the first ninety seconds. Davis had a three-point play, and Flowers III hit a three-pointer to extend the ACU lead to 11 points at 49–38 with 16:42 left in the game.

In the next nine minutes of play, the Seahawks cut the lead to 5 points on six different occasions, but the Firestorm was able to answer back with points of its own. Marko Radulovic made both free throws with 7:41 left to cut the ACU lead to 66–61. AJ turned back the Seahawks with 3 free throws to push the lead to 8. ACU was able to put the game on ice by hitting 9 of 12 free throws in the last three-plus minutes to beat the host school 85–76.

ACU had nine players score 6 or more points. AJ finished the night going 6 for 8 from the floor and 18 points. "It was great coming back to my home state and playing games," AJ recalled of this trip. "I just felt more calm and peaceful." Marcus Green scored 12 points in twelve minutes of play. Wilson had 7 points and 6 rebounds. Pat Fisher had 6 points and 4 assists. Core'Von Lott led all scorers with 24 points for Keiser, while his teammate Quinton Glaspie had 20 points and 6 rebounds. The loss left Keiser with a 3-and-3 record, while ACU improved to 7 and 1.

November 24, 2021
Student Life Center,
West Palm Beach, Florida
Florida Memorial College Lions

The Thanksgiving Eve matchup was a tall order for the Firestorm. The Lions had four seven-foot players on its roster. ACU's Bryce Davis is 6'7," and Robby Wilson is listed at 6'9." The Lions entered the game at 5 and 4 on the season.

ACU got off to a better start offensively for the first time in several games. The Firestorm was up 11 to 4 with just over sixteen minutes left in the half when Mubashar Ali scored 7 straight points for Florida Memorial to make the score 14–11 ACU. The Firestorm then stopped the Lions on 9 straight possessions and went on a 13-to-0 run. ACU was now up 27–11 with 8:30 left in the half. Bryce Davis went 6 for 6 from the free throw line during that stretch.

A layup by Marcus Green and a three-pointer by AJ extended the lead to 20 points with seven minutes before the half, 32–12. The ACU defense only allowed 1 point in ten minutes of play. Arizona Christian was able to cruise to a 42–19 halftime lead. Florida Memorial only shot 23 percent from the floor and 1–12 (8.3%) from three-point range. Meanwhile, ACU shot 57 percent from the floor and made 15 of 17 free throws in the first half.

In the locker room, Coach Rutter pointed out the poor shooting by Florida Memorial, and that they would make shots in the second half. "We need to keep playing solid defense and keep their big guys from getting offensive rebounds."

The Firestorm kept on rolling in the second half, expanding the lead to 25 points several times. With just under six minutes to play, Dennis Flowers III hit back-to-back three-pointers. AJ and Davis made layups, and AJ made free throws to put ACU up 75–44 with just over three minutes left. The Firestorm was able to win by 24 points, 79–55.

The coach in the ACU locker room with the biggest smile on his face was Coach J.O. This was his second scout of the year; his first was the blowout win over SAGU. "When we walked into the gym, Florida Memorial was humongous," Coach J.O. commented. "We had a nice halftime lead, and our defense was able to keep the Lions' leading scorer of the year scoreless in the game."

Florida Memorial was able to shoot better in the second half to finish the game at 36 percent from the floor and 25 percent from long range. Mubashar Ali came off the bench to lead the Lions with 12 points. ACU had five players in double figures and were 25 of 29 (86%) from the free throw line. AJ with 16, Davis 14, Marcus Green 11, Flowers and Goudeau had 10 points each.

"This was the game I really feel as a team we were able to figure it out," Robby Wilson added.

After the game, the team traveled in vans to the Don Shula Hotel in Miami. Shortly after we arrived, Coach Rutter gave the team a quick NFL history lesson on the Hall of Fame Coach Don Shula. Coach Vande Zande and Coach Rutter were the only two on the team who remembered the Dolphins being a powerhouse for years in the NFL with Shula as the head coach.

Thanksgiving Day
November 25, 2021
Miami, Florida

"This is the day the Lord has made;
Let us rejoice and be glad in it"
(Psalm 118:24).

This was not a typical Thanksgiving Day for the members of the Arizona Christian University basketball team. For the first time in their lives, many of the team players and coaches were away from their immediate families. Instead, they were with their basketball family. The day started at nine o'clock with a morning stretch and some light shooting. Another activity that didn't make this a traditional Thanksgiving Day was a trip to Miami Beach. Four basketball coaches, Transformational Coach Chambers, and six players made the adventure to Miami Beach on a cloudy and cooler day for a swim in the Atlantic Ocean. Coach Chambers doesn't travel with the basketball team, but Coach Chambers also serves as chaplain on weekends for the Carolina Panthers. The Panthers were in Miami for the weekend, so Coach Chambers was able to minister to both teams. Most of the participants took off their shoes and made a mad dash into the waves of the Atlantic Ocean—even the oldest, Coach V.

"My goal every time I swim in the ocean," Coach Oetjen proclaimed, "is to swim far enough off the coast to get the lifeguard to blow the whistle at me!"

Lo and behold, and it wasn't long before: *Phooweet!* "Hey, you're not supposed to swim that far out!" the lifeguard yelled out of the megaphone. Needless to say, that made many of us chuckle. That was typical of

Coach O. He is definitely a risk-taker. Coach O. was also one of the first guys to volunteer to go first on the ropes course events back in September. As Coach O. swam back to the shallower water, a big smile was on his face. "See what I mean!"

After swimming and crashing in the waves for about an hour, we dried off and walked back to where we parked. Before heading back, a few players found a burger-and-shake diner. No one could pass on such a meal.

After a practice at St. Thomas University, Coach Welty drove to a nearby Cracker Barrel Restaurant to get our name down for reservations. It was going to be a two-hour wait for a party of twenty-two. Coach Welty found a nearby coffee shop; he hunkered down and watched game film until his number was called.

Meanwhile, the team went back to the Don Shula Hotel, hung out, watched NFL football, and waited to get the call from Coach Welty to travel to the restaurant.

When we arrived at the restaurant, there was a huge line of cars driving through for take-out orders. Our team vans had to park at nearby businesses to find a place to park.

Once inside Cracker Barrel, the team sat around two large tables. Most of the team ordered the traditional Thanksgiving Day meal special of turkey, potatoes, stuffing, cornbread, choice of vegetable, and pumpkin pie. Some players ordered breakfast meals or steaks. The service was outstanding. Lots of stories and laughter were heard and seen throughout the hour we were there.

If one needs to be away from family on Thanksgiving Day, spending time with a basketball family is an excellent alternative. Robby Wilson agreed, "This is the first time I have been away from family at Thanksgiving, but spending time with the team makes it feel like family. We just needed to lean on each other."

Coach Welty and Coach O.

November 26, 2021
Fernandez Family Center
Miami, Florida
St. Thomas University Bobcats (STU)

The third and final game in four days had the 8–1 fourth-ranked Firestorm against the tall and athletic 2–3 Bobcats of St. Thomas University. This was predicted to be the toughest competition for ACU on the Florida trip. Coach Chambers was able to lead a short devotional before the final scout and instructions before the warmups started.

The home team started out hot and took a 7–1 lead with just two minutes into the game. A three-pointer by Wilson and layups by AJ and Bradford pulled the Firestorm into an 8–8 tie with just under fifteen minutes left in the half. The teams battled to a tie eight different times until the score was tied at 23 with 6:38 left until intermission.

Darius Goudeau for ACU connected from long range twice in the final five minutes of the first half. His second three gave the Firestorm a 33–31 lead with two minutes left. In the closing ninety seconds, St. Thomas made one free throw, and nailed a long bomb from Jonas Parker with just ten seconds before halftime. St. Thomas regained the momentum 35–33 heading into the locker room.

Both teams shot 40 percent from the floor in the first half and 36 percent from long range. STU had 19 rebounds and with 4 offensive rebounds (a big focus for the game. STU was averaging around 15 offensive rebounds per game). The Bobcats had 7 turnovers. Meanwhile, ACU had 12 boards and one turnover. Jonas Parker had 16 points at the half for STU, while Goudeau had 8 points, and freshman Marcus Green had 7 for ACU.

Dennis Flowers hit a three-pointer fifteen seconds into the second half to lift the Firestorm to a 36–35 lead. The lead was short-lived. The Bobcats went on a 10–0 run in the next four minutes. Now STU was up 45–36. The Firestorm failed to score on 9 straight possessions. During the scoring drought for ACU, Point Guard AJ got elbowed in the head and needed to leave the game with 15:45 in the half. A trail of blood followed AJ off the floor and into a nearby bathroom. "I know I got cracked on the forehead pretty good," AJ said after the game. "I checked to see if there was any blood, and yeah, there was a lot. Just needed to get off the floor and get help."

While AJ was getting attended to in the training room, Backup Point Guard Pat Fisher filled in. Fisher's contribution for ACU was felt right away as he scored two layups in one minute. The Firestorm was now down 45–40 with 14:07 left in the game. The scoring woes continued in the second half. Then Fisher had to leave the game with a finger injury with just under ten minutes to play. KeyVaughn Williams now would take over as the point guard. Coach V. made his way to the training room to check on AJ's situation. The trainer said, "We will put butterfly bandages on the cut on his forehead, wrap it up, and let him finish the game. He will need to get stitches before you fly back to Arizona."

When AJ checked back in with 8:34 left in the game with a bandage on his forehead, ACU was down 54–43. His timing was perfect because the team needed a spark, and AJ delivered! The Firestorm scored on 4 of its next 5 possessions and a 10–0 run starting with an offensive putback by Marcus Green.

Green would have another basket, while Flowers III had points, and AJ had a layup to cut the deficit to 1 at 54–53, STU in the lead with 5:43 to play. "When I came back in the game from the trainer's room, we were down," AJ recalled. "I just wanted to bring some energy to our team."

Jonas Parker scored for STU with three minutes left to give a five-point lead for the home team at 60–55. AJ followed that up with a layup, and Flowers nailed a three-pointer as the shot clock was running out. The score was now STU 61–60 with 1:44 left. The Bobcats had several opportunities to extend the lead, but they failed to make free throws or shots.

With :71 left in the game and leading by 1, the Bobcats called a timeout. STU inbounded the ball under its own basket; they tried a lob pass, which was thrown too high, and the errant pass ended up in the hands of speedy ACU's Angelo Johnson. AJ raced to the other end of the court for an uncontested layup and a 62–61 Firestorm lead. It was the first lead for ACU since the opening minute of the second half.

That would prove to be the final score. Neither team was able to score in the final minute. STU had several shots to regain the lead, and ACU had a charge called and a turnover down the stretch. The turnover was a free violation on ACU with :09 left. So, with nine ticks on the clock left and no time-outs left, the Bobcats inbounded the ball with one last attempt to pull the game out. STU had a tough time executing what play was called from the bench, thanks to the stingy Firestorm defense. The Bobcats did get a long-range three-pointer from Jonas Parker that came up short off the front of the rim at the buzzer. ACU survived with a 62–61 road victory.

ACU was fortunate to come away with the victory and improved to 9–1 on the year. St. Thomas finished the game with 19 offensive rebounds and 52 total rebounds, but they turned the ball over 16 times. ACU had 33 total rebounds and turned the ball over 9 times. Jonas Parker led the Bobcats with 20 points. Flowers led the Firestorm with 16, and Marcus Green with 13 points and 5 boards. AJ finished with 10 points and 3 steals, but he lifted and inspired the team with his reentry into the game after the cut on his forehead. The tall STU men inside limited ACU big men Davis to 4 points and Wilson to 3.

In the locker room after the game, Coach Rutter made a few announcements. "We need to make this quick. Congratulations on the win. I am not sure how we were able to pull that off. I am proud of your determination and effort to battle against this team. We have less than three hours to clean up, get AJ to a clinic for stitches, stop for something to eat, fuel up the rental vans, and drive to the airport. Let's pray."

Now that the game was over, the race was on! Thank the Lord that Coach Chambers was staying in Miami for the weekend for the Panthers/ Dolphins game. Coach Chambers dropped Coach V. and AJ off at a nearby

Urgent Care clinic that the STU trainer had contacted for us to get speedy help. Coach Chambers would come back and pick us up to take us to the airport after he took a van-load of other players to the airport.

After about forty-five minutes at the Urgent Care, AJ came out with seven stitches. "At the clinic, they numbed my forehead some," AJ admitted. "But I could still feel the stitches being pulled tight when they were finishing up."

Coach Chambers showed up in a few minutes to take AJ and Coach V. to the airport. Since Coach Chambers was using this rental van for the weekend, he just dropped AJ and Coach V. at the terminal. Coach Welty met AJ and Coach V. by the ticket area, and we were escorted to the front of the line for the TSA security check. We made it to our gate with about fifteen minutes to spare. It was now on to Chicago and then to Phoenix. The plane touched down just before midnight at Sky Harbor Airport in Phoenix. That was quite the whirlwind of a day.

The Firestorm basketball team had won three games against much taller teams in four days on the road, and everyone with our team was back in Phoenix before the clock struck midnight. "This was such a long road trip," Paul Hayden recalled. It was a pivotal time for our team as we drew closer as a team, and we learned how to play together."

This was a chance for the team to grow closer together by spending a lot of time with one another, experiencing new adventures, and spending a major holiday as a team away from the friendly confines of home. Thanksgiving 2021 will be remembered for many years by all of those who made the trip, and by the families who missed loved ones on Thanksgiving Day.

Coach Chambers had this reaction to what he witnessed during the St. Thomas game:

"We will never forget our Thanksgiving journey to Florida. We were playing against a very talented St. Thomas team at their place in Miami. The game was lightly attended, but what took place on the floor was an incredible demonstration of Christ-like attitude and effort in competition. In Arizona Christian basketball, we pride ourselves to honor Jesus because the game of basketball was created for Him.

"In the second half of the highly contested game, Angelo Johnson drove to the hoop and was elbowed in the head. As I sat on our bench, I watched AJ run the entire floor, spilling blood across the entire court on his way back to the bench. Play was stopped to clean the floor. I could not help but think of the blood of Jesus and the price He paid for us. The trainer from the other team was willing to help AJ to get his bleeding stopped. She served him as if he was one of her own players. It was a profound example of servant leadership glorifying Jesus in the midst of athletic competition.

"Jesus saves us through the shedding of His blood, and an opposing trainer from another team 'saved' ACU basketball by stopping AJ's blood, which allowed him to be 'resurrected' to return to the floor to finish the game. We watched AJ embody his typical calm, cool, and collected demeanor, while his actions spoke the resolve and passion of Christ fueling our team to prevail. In seventeen years of ministry, it was one of the greatest demonstrations of competing for Jesus Christ that we have ever seen."

The team had Saturday and Sunday off. Two strong GSAC opponents were coming to Arizona for games on Thursday, December 2, and Saturday, December 4. On Monday, it was announced that AJ was awarded the GSAC Player of the Week for his strong performance in his home state of Florida over the Thanksgiving week. AJ and Pat were both held out of practice—AJ with the injury to his head, and Pat with his injured middle finger on his left hand. Pat would have a hand specialist look at the finger on Thursday. This injury to Pat would have a ripple effect on the team for the rest of the season.

CHAPTER 9

IT'S THE MOST WONDERFUL TIME OF THE YEAR

"For unto us a child is born, to us a Son is given, and the government shall be on His shoulders. And He will be called Wonderful, Counselor, Mighty God, Everlasting Father, Prince of Peace" (Isaiah 9:6).

When the calendar switches to December, many start thinking more about Christmas and the Advent season. It is also time during the basketball season that teams will play some meaningful games before the semester's end and Christmas break.

December 2, 2022
The Events Center
Glendale, Arizona
Westmont College, Montecito, California

Early in the afternoon, Coach V. drove AJ to a clinic to have the stitches on his forehead removed, and we returned to campus thirty minutes before the walk-through and shoot-around for the game that night. AJ was cleared to play, but Pat would not be playing tonight or for the next eight weeks. His left middle finger sustained ligament damage in the game against St. Thomas. When asked how he hurt the finger, Pat responded with, "All I did was swat down on the ball, and when I looked at my finger, it was just hanging there." Pat was doing a fantastic job at relieving AJ at the point guard position early in the season. There is a cliché in sports when a player goes down to injury or cannot compete: "Next man up!" The next man up was KeyVaughn Williams. He was now the backup point guard, and he would get his first opportunity in his new role in a few hours.

Before the game against Westmont, Coach Rutter was presented with a team-signed basketball from Athletic Director Pete Dryer for Coach Rutter's 200th win at ACU, which was accomplished earlier in the season.

Westmont entered the game undefeated (8–0 and 1–0 in GSAC) and were receiving votes in the latest NAIA poll. ACU is the NAIA's sixth-ranked team at 9–1 overall and 1–1 in GSAC.

With the game just three minutes old, Bryce Davis made a layup to tie the score at 4. Westmont would spend the next five minutes outscoring ACU 14 to 2. The Firestorm was down 12 points, 18–6, with 12:27 left to play until half. Maybe it was the effects of the long trip away to Florida, but the ACU defense looked like Swiss cheese with many holes in it. Westmont's Nate Meithof and Ajay Singh were nearly scoring at will.

The Firestorm was able to mount its own 13–4 run to pull within 3 points at 22–19 with just under eight minutes to play before the break. ACU got a 3 from Gonzalez, 5 points from Flowers III, and baskets by Davis and AJ.

The Warriors' Singh and Meithof continued to lead the scoring attack as Westmont regained a twelve-point advantage, 31–19, with just over five minutes to halftime. Westmont was able to maintain a double-digit lead at the half, 42–32.

"For a team that prides itself on solid defense, we sure are not getting it done tonight, fellas," Coach Rutter commented to the team in the locker room. Westmont was shooting 50 percent from the floor, and Singh had 14 points, and Meithof had 12 at the break. Flowers III had 10 for ACU, while the Firestorm shot only 35 percent from the floor.

The Firestorm came out of the lull in the second half and cut into the deficit quickly. A three-pointer by Flowers III in its first possession started a 10–1 run. That was followed up with baskets by Davis and AJ. Micah Bradford made a three-pointer to make the score 43–42, Westmont still holding on to the lead with 17:30 left.

Now, it was Westmont that went on a scoring binge while ACU struggled to score. The Warriors led by 14 points, 58–44, with 13:53 left to play. Westmont was able to maintain the lead over the Firestorm behind the scoring of Singh and Cade Roth.

With 10:23 left in the game and the Firestorm trailing by 9, Key Williams took advantage of the extended playing he got because of the injury to Pat Fisher. In the next five minutes, Williams would score 9 points, including some acrobatic layups and a huge three-pointer, with 3:22 to play, which pulled the Firestorm to within 4 points, 75–71. Dom Gonzalez made it a one-point game, 75–74, when he connected from long range and 2:40 to play.

Bryce Davis was able to tie the score at 77 when he made one of two free throws. There was just 1:25 left to play. Gonzalez got the offensive rebound on the missed free throw, but Flowers III's potential go-ahead basket did not fall.

Westmont called a timeout with just over a minute left. There was a lot of excitement in the ACU huddle. The team had played a poor first half defensively and had fought back from several second-half deficits to be in a position to pull out the game. One could see in the players' eyes and body language that it was a confident group who felt they could get the job done. "We just need one defensive stop, and we will get our chance to get the win," Coach Rutter reminded the team. "Make sure to box out!"

After working the ball around the perimeter for around ten seconds, Westmont's Cade Roth drove to the left elbow and made a contested jumper; plus he was fouled on the play. Roth made the free throw to put Westmont up 80–77 with :37 left.

Coach Rutter called a time-out. ACU's Key Williams was not able to make his shot attempt, and Roth got the defensive rebound for Westmont. He was fouled immediately by Davis.

Roth missed the first free throw of the bonus situation, and Davis brought down the rebound for ACU. AJ was not able to connect on a tough layup with :12 left. Westmont got the rebound and called a thirty-second time-out. ACU then used a full time-out. ACU was down 80–77, and still a chance to force a tie if they could get a defensive stop.

Westmont's Jared Brown was fouled with five seconds on a drive to the basket. Brown was able to ice the victory by making both free throws, 82–77. AJ was able to nail an uncontested three-pointer as the final horn sounded to make it an 82–80 final score.

Wow, the preseason GSAC favorite ACU was 1–2 after three games played. Westmont was 2–0 and shot close to 50 percent from the floor for the game. "We played tonight like we practiced all week," Coach Rutter said to a very somber locker room. "The effort on defense was not at a championship level. This will be a tough learning experience for us. Give Westmont credit. They had an answer for every run that we made at them throughout the game."

Singh finished with a game-high 24 points, Meithof had 20, Jared Brown 15, Kyler Warren had 10, while Roth had 9 points and 10 rebounds. Westmont's starters had all but 4 points for the Warriors.

"It's a big feat to win in that kind of fashion in their place," a jubilant Westmont Coach Landon Boucher commented after the win. "They play really well at home, and they are not just talented, but they are deep as well. Our guys put together a gutsy effort. There were times down the stretch where it would have been easy to give up. ACU made run after run in the second half, but our guys stuck with it and stayed together."

Flowers III finished with 15; Marcus Green played well again offensively by scoring 13 points in eleven minutes of play.

Key Williams responded like the coaches thought he would with extended playing time. He ended the night with 12 points going 5 for 6 from the field and 2 of 2 from the line, and he added 5 assists to ignite the second half comeback for ACU. "I was ready to play some significant minutes tonight," Williams shared after the game. "It was a moment to prove myself. We were down in the game, and we needed a spark. I was glad I could contribute."

AJ finished with 11 points. Dom Gonzalez went 3 for 4 from deep for 9 points.

"Watching us lose to Westmont really struck a nerve with me," Bowers added. "I wasn't playing yet, and I still wasn't one-hundred percent sure if I was going to red-shirt or not."

After such a rough start to the conference season, Coach Chambers texted, "We Rise Again!"

Coach Welty texted out: "Consistency Compounds: All that compounding results in surprising 'leaps.'"

Coach Rutter presented 200th victory ball by Athletic Director Pete Dryer

December 4, 2021
The Events Center
Glendale, Arizona
The Master's University/Santa Clarita, California

This Saturday afternoon GSAC matchup featured the top-fifteen-ranked NAIA teams.

The Master's University was ranked 12th, while the Firestorm was ranked 6th. The Mustangs were coming off a three-point overtime win on Thursday night over Ottawa University. Meanwhile, ACU was looking forward to playing again to rid themselves of the loss versus Westmont on Thursday night.

The defensive focus was to keep the Mustangs out of the lane and to have better shot selection. In the loss to Westmont, Coach Rutter learned by watching the film of the game that ACU shot too many three-pointers early in the shot clock. He wanted the team to show better discipline and patience.

The game got off to a sluggish start as both teams struggled to find the bottom of the net. ACU's Bryce Davis scored the first two baskets for the Firestorm. Robby Wilson added a three-pointer with just under fifteen minutes left in the half to give ACU a 7–6 lead.

Marcus Green hit a jumper with nine minutes left in the first half to give the Firestorm a 14–12 lead—a lead they would not give back. As a matter of fact, TMU would only score 8 more points before halftime. Meanwhile, the Firestorm got balanced scoring with putting up another 21 points before the teams went to regroup in their locker rooms. ACU was up 35–20. The Mustangs had 12 turnovers at the break while shooting only 29 percent from the floor. ACU was shooting 40 percent from the floor, but seven different players scored in the first twenty minutes.

ACU continued to build on its halftime lead when Davis scored 4 straight points to push the lead to 39–20 with 18:19 left in the game. A minute later, Flowers III scored a layup to give the Firestorm its biggest lead of the afternoon, 41–20. ACU was able bring home a 70-57 victory over the Mustangs.

"We struggled to remain composed in the first half, which led to excessive turnovers," Master's Head Coach Kelvin Starr stated after the game. "Can't let a team as talented as ACU get a fifteen-point lead at the half. It was too much of an uphill battle."

Arizona Christian was able to maintain a comfortable lead throughout the second half as TMU struggled to score and turned the ball over twenty-three times for the game. The Firestorm went 8 for 8 from the free throw line in the last few minutes, allowing ACU to ice the victory 70–57.

"That was not a pretty win, but it was a good team win with many players making contributions," commented Coach Rutter after seeing his team go 2–2 in league play. "We looked a lot more like ourselves today. Defensively better, and shot selection was much improved. I think we're a little worn out from a couple weeks of travel, some injuries, and not many practices leading up to the Westmont game. Our fundamentals slipped because of that."

Davis led the home team with 13 points and 7 boards. Flowers III and Wilson had 11 apiece. The ACU bench scored 27 points, with Paul Hayden scoring 10 points in eight minutes of play, going 3 of 4 from the floor. "I felt in the groove right away coming off the bench," Hayden responded after the game. Dom Gonzalez scored 9 points and 3 steals. ACU also shot 77 percent from the free throw line going 27–35.

The team had Sunday off, like usual, and Monday, December 7, was a film session on the Westmont and Master's game. The players also did some shooting before or after the film session. Tuesday was a preparation day for our game against Ottawa University, which is located in Surprise, Arizona, a mere twenty-five-minute drive west from ACU. Coach Welty had the scout for this game since he was familiar with the coaching staff at Ottawa. The head coach, Matt Keely, was an assistant coach at MidAmerica Nazarene University in Kansas when Coach Welty played there a few seasons ago.

During Wednesday's practice, Dennis Flowers fell and hurt his hip, while Darius Goudeau landed awkwardly under the basket and hurt his foot. Their playing status was questionable.

December 9, 2021
Faith Arena
Surprise, Arizona
Ottawa University (OUAZ) Spirit

Coach Welty's message to the team was, "The greatest opponent: *ourselves*. Don't waste energy or focus on who we compete against tonight. Bring an edge that competes for our individual and collective potential."

Coach Welty had the scout against Ottawa. "I had some extra juice with scouting my former assistant coach, Matt Keeley, from my playing days in Kansas," Coach Welty added. "It is always fun to play against guys you've known your entire life, and coupled with the emerging rivalry from the west side of town made it fun."

The much-anticipated GSAC–Arizona rivalry game was pivotal for both teams on this Thursday night in December in the

Desert. OUAZ entered the game confident with a 7–3 record and 2–2 in GSAC. The Spirit had beaten NCAA Division 1 Denver University earlier in the year. Last weekend, they split their GSAC games, losing in overtime to The Master's and beating Westmont. ACU was 10–2 on the year and 2–2 in league play.

The sixth-ranked Firestorm would be down two players with injuries. Pat Fisher was out for two months with a finger ligament injury. Darius Goudeau hurt his foot on Wednesday in practice. Starting Guard Dennis Flowers III would be limited with a hip injury.

The early stages of the contest saw several lead changes and ties. OUAZ went up 12–5 after a three-point basket by Kolton Hitt with just under fifteen minutes to play. The Firestorm then went on a 13–6 run to tie the score at 18. Paul Hayden scored 7 of ACU points in that run. There were still ten minutes left in the half.

Two times before half, the Spirit was able to take a six-point lead. Hayden was able to tie the score at 31 with a layup and just over two minutes until intermission. The score was tied again at 33 with :22 before half.

After a turnover by Ottawa with :04 left, Coach Rutter subbed in KeyVaughn Williams to inbound the ball. The Firestorm had the full ninety-four feet to work with to get a go-ahead basket. On a called full-court out-of-bounds play, Williams's bullet of a pass landed in AJ's hands as he streaked down the left sideline in front of OUAZ's bench. The speedster was able to lay the ball over two defenders waiting for him at the rim. The ball caromed high off the glass and through the net as time expired. AJ slid across the Faith Arena floor as ACU took the momentum and a 35–33 lead into the locker room at halftime. The team sprinted off the bench to help get AJ off the floor and trot into the locker room.

The first half lived up to its billing as a much-anticipated game. The halftime statistics were similar for both teams. Each team had some offensive runs, which gave the game several momentum swings in the first twenty minutes.

The Firestorm picked up where it left off to end the half by scoring the first 7 points of the second half. Four points from Davis, a free throw by AJ, and a layup by Gonzalez made the score 42–33 with 16:19 left in the game. Paul Hayden and Marcus Green each hit three-pointers to extend the lead to 12 at 50–38 with just under thirteen minutes left. Green also added a baseline double-clutch highlight dunk to put ACU up 52–42 with just over eleven minutes to play.

Ottawa was not going anywhere, as Jayce Catchings tallied 5 straight points to cut the lead to 5 at 60–55 with 7:30 until the final horn. Micah Bradford answered with a three-pointer for ACU 63–55, now 7:10 to play. A minute and a half later, with the shot clock running out, Bryce Davis attempted his first three-pointer of the year! *Swish*, nothing but net. The Firestorm bench erupted with loud cheers as the team stretched the lead to 8 again.

Kolton Hitt and Devin Collins pulled OUAZ back to within 3 points at the 3:36 mark, and the score was 70–67. Neither team was able to score for the next two minutes of play.

Another big man for ACU hit another 3. This time, Wilson was given a great pass from AJ, and Robby buried it with 1:21 left and a six-point advantage at 73–67.

Ottawa's big man Josiah De'Lacerda hit a jumper to cut the lead to 4 with just under a minute to play, 73–69. AJ made one of two free throws to make it a five-point lead with :21. OUAZ's Marcus Williams hit a long 3 to cut the lead to 2 with :10.

ACU inbounded the ball to Dom Gonzalez, who was fouled, and he walked slowly and confidently to the other end and drained both free throws to ice the victory 76–72. Gonzalez's boldness goes back to his high school days at Ironwood High School in Glendale, Arizona. Dom learned then to think and say to himself, "You fouled the wrong shooter!"

"Great win for us. Really proud how our guys battled," a smiling Coach Rutter said after the Phoenix area rivalry win. "We had multiple guys out with injuries and had several players in foul trouble in both halves. Our three freshmen, Dom, Paul, and Marcus, were really good tonight and played fearless. Key was big as usual in a big game, and AJ was good on both ends. Also we have three bigs that can be a special front for us with Robby, Davis, and Bowers."

The ACU bench has been strong all year, and tonight, it outscored OUAZ 37–20. "The guys coming off the bench have the mindset there are no breaks," Paul Hayden stated. "We are still getting after it!" Hayden finished with 12, Green with 11, and Gonzalez with 6, including the free throws that closed the door on the Spirit. KeyVaughn had 6 points and 5 assists. Davis led all ACU scorers with 13 going 5 of 6 from the floor and 5 boards. Wilson and AJ both had 11. Dennis

Flowers III only played twelve minutes with his sore hip.

OUAZ had a balanced scoring attack with Jayce Catchings leading the way with 15 points in sixteen minutes of play off the bench. Hitt and De'Lacerda had 14 each, Collins had 12, while Malbough had 10. Ottawa is now 2–3 in GSAC and ACU improved to 3–2 in the conference. It was a short, sweet ride home to Glendale after a quick stop at an In & Out Burger restaurant. The Firestorm's next game would be in eight days at the Cactus Classic in Chandler-Gilbert, Arizona. It was time for semester finals week.

CHAPTER 10

CACTUS CLASSIC

"Do not be afraid. I bring you good news of a great joy that will be for all people. Today a Savior has been to you; He is Christ the Lord" (Luke 2:10–11).

December 17, 2021
Cactus Classic
Coyote Center Chandler-Gilbert
Community College
Chandler, Arizona
Carroll College Saints
Helena, Montana

In their first game in eight days, ACU was matched up against Carroll College of Montana, the team that knocked the Firestorm out of the NAIA tournament last March in the second round. This game was anticipated by both teams, and it was a top-ten matchup between second-ranked Carroll College Saints and the tenth-ranked Firestorm. Both teams had most of their players back from last season's teams.

It was also the opportunity for Dennis Flowers III to face the team he played for last season. He transferred to ACU during the summer. "I was really excited to play my former teammates," Flowers III admitted. His hip injury was improved with the eight days of rest. Also on the injury front, Pat would be out until early February. Darius Goudeau ended up bruising his plantar fascia, and he would be out indefinitely. This injury now changed the status of Xander Bowers. The thought of redshirting him was over. Bowers had sat out several games and played in a few. With Pat and Darius out, Bowers would be needed more than ever. Shaun Wahlstrom had a head injury from practice earlier in the week but was cleared to play.

The game could not have started any worse for Arizona Christian. Carroll jumped out to an early 10–0 lead as ACU had 2 turnovers in its first 4 possessions. Coach Rutter used a thirty-second time-out. "We need to do a better job of closing out on the shooters," Coach Rutter said calmly. "Stick to the game plan, and be patient on offense."

Xander Bowers checked into the game during the time-out, and he scored right away to give the Firestorm its first points. Bryce Davis scored 5 points in a 9–0 run to pull the Firestorm within 1 at 10–9 with 14:16 left in the half.

The teams continued to battle back and forth with neither team getting a large lead. There were several ties along the way and several lead changes. The game was tied at 34 at the half.

For a game that was billed to be a classic with two evenly matched teams, the first half answered that question. Both teams had scoring runs; there were lead changes and several ties. The halftime statistics were fairly even. Bryce Davis had 9 points and Dom Gonzalez had 6 for ACU, while Gui Pedra had 8 points and Shamrock Campbell had 7.

Campbell had ended the first half with the last basket made, and he picked up where he left off by hitting a three-pointer to start the second half. That gave the Saints an early three-point lead. Two times in the second half, the Saints were able to lead by 5.

ACU was able to wrestle the lead away from Carroll and take its own five-point lead after free throws by Wilson and a jumper by Paul Hayden. It was now 49–44 ACU with 13:24 to play. The teams continued to battle for the lead, and Carroll took another four-point lead with 7:36 left in the game on a basket by Jovan Šljvančanin.

With 5:39 on the clock, Key Williams made a beautiful pass, which led to a Xander

Bowers dunk and another tie score at 61. After Bryce Davis made one of two free throws and a 64–63 lead with just over three minutes to play, Carroll's Brendan Temple made a basket to give the lead back to the Saints 65–64 with 1:55 left.

After Shamrock Campbell missed a shot with just under a minute to play and Carroll clinging to a one-point lead, Coach Rutter called a time-out as ACU had rebounded the missed shot attempt. Dom Gonzalez was inserted into the lineup. Again, not much panic in the Firestorm huddle; just confidence that someone on the team will get a great shot on this possession.

With :40 on the clock, AJ drove the left baseline and fired a bullseye pass to Gonzalez in the right corner. Dom hit nothing but net on the shot. His teammates right behind him on the bench exploded with joyful cheers to celebrate the big shot and a 67–65 lead. "I really wanted to shoot that shot!" Dom shared after the game. "The moment is not too big."

Coach Rutter called another time-out to reinsert Bowers back in the lineup for his outstanding defensive skills.

Trailing by two points, Carroll did not go to its sharp-shooting Campbell or Jovan, who is a great scorer in the lane, but instead, the Saints got the ball to Ifeanyi Okeke. Okeke caught the ball with his back to the basket about eight feet from the rim off the right block. Being guarded by Robby Wilson, Okeke faked to his right shoulder and then spun around to his left. He elevated over Wilson and hit the game-tying shot with :21 left, and the game tied at 67. Carroll called a time-out.

Arizona Christian would have the chance to win the game on its last possession. Everyone in our huddle knew that Angelo Johnson would be taking the last shot unless some breakdown happened by the Carroll defense. As ACU brought the ball up the floor, the crowd at the Coyote Center came to their feet, and cellphone cameras were recording. AJ got the ball at the top of the circle with about ten seconds left. He slowly and carefully dribbled over to the left sideline, and, with about three ticks left on the clock, he broke and weaved his way to the hoop. The Carroll defense waited for him there, so AJ was forced to attempt a difficult reverse layup. He made it just like he does in practice frequently. "Actually, I was thinking of pulling up for a short jumper, but I saw the defender's feet. I knew I could get by him," AJ commented later. The Firestorm fans and team rejoiced as ACU took a 69–67 lead and a hard-fought victory. The Firestorm players ran onto the court to rejoice on the big win over Carroll. "It was a fun game to play in, and it felt really good to beat them," AJ admitted. "But it still doesn't erase what happened last year!"

People in attendance that late Friday afternoon witnessed a great well-played college basketball game—an early Christmas treat. A game that featured 15 lead changes and 9 ties. ACU had 7 turnovers and shot over 52 percent from the floor. Carroll had 10 turnovers and shot 52 percent from three-point land. Both teams had 13 fouls called on them, so there were not many free throws taken.

The Firestorm had four players in double figures. AJ finished with 13 points and 3 assists, Wilson had 12, and Davis had 11. All three of those players had 4 rebounds too. The ACU bench scored 27 points with Gonzalez scoring 10 points and Bowers with 6 points and 4 rebounds. Flowers III was able to score 4 points and grab 3 rebounds against this former team. His stingy defense also was a key in the win for ACU. "I knew that Carroll would be keyed on slowing me down offensively," Flowers III confessed after the game. "The win is a testament to how balanced our team is."

Campbell led all scorers with 17 points, Hillman had 12, and Jovan had 10 points and 10 rebounds for the Saints.

A joyful Coach Rutter had these observations after the win: "We had a great week of practice, and we really improved. Carroll does not beat themselves and does not make many mistakes. We challenged our guys to stay focused and keep fighting. Our shot selection was really good, and we executed down the stretch. Dom hit another huge shot, and AJ made big plays."

The loss was the first of the season for Carroll, 12–1, while ACU improved to 12–2.

December 18, 2021
Cactus Classic
Coyote Center
Chandler-Gilbert Community College
Chandler, Arizona
Rocky Mountain College Bears
Billings, Montana

The biggest fear of any coach in any sport after a highly anticipated game is how the team will play in the next game. After the thrilling seesaw battle the night before, ACU was playing its second game in less than twenty-four hours against Rocky Mountain College.

Senior Captain Robby Wilson helped ACU get off to a solid start. Wilson did his part by scoring the first 4 points for the Firestorm. After baskets by Flowers III and Davis, Wilson scored his sixth point of the night to put his team up 10–6 with 16:42 left in the half.

With a 22–19 lead with just over ten minutes left in the half, ACU went on a 13–0 run to push the lead to 35–19 with 7:21 left before half. Rocky Mountain was not able to cut into the deficit before half as ACU maintained a 16-point advantage of 47–31.

In the second half, both teams traded baskets, and after two free throws by Micah Bradford, ACU was up 54–38. Bryce Davis went on a personal seven-point scoring run for ACU to extend the lead to 60–42.

With just under ten minutes to play, Jesse Owens hit a three-pointer for the Bears to cut the lead to 65–50. A layup and back-to-back dunks by ACU's Bowers extended the lead to 71–52 with 8:30 left in the game. The ACU lead was extended to 25 points with three-pointers coming from AJ, Bradford, and Flowers III 84–59 with just under five minutes to play.

ACU was able to get Chris Daniels and Shaun Wahlstrom into the game in the last five minutes, and they helped salt away the game for a 90–69 win.

Abdul Bah led the Bears with 14 points, and his team dropped to 5–6 on the season. Robby Wilson had a double-double with 17 points and 15 rebounds. Davis had 16 points and 6 boards, Bradford had 11, and Hayden had 10 points. ACU out-rebounded Rocky Mountain 50–25 and improved to 13–2.

"This was a huge win for us," Wilson commented after the game. "We had a big win last night, and we didn't have a letdown. We beat a solid team tonight, so this is a big confidence booster for us going forward."

"Robby, Xander, and Bryce were big on the offensive glass, and it helped open the game up," Coach Rutter praised the three bigs after the game. "I thought we were a little flat to start off the game after a quick turnaround. We settled down and defensively tightened up. Also, we were able to get our transition game going."

December 20. 2021
Coyote Center
Chandler-Gilbert Community College
Chandler, Arizona
Montana State-Northern Stars/
Havre, Montana

In its final game before taking a much-deserved Christmas break, ACU would face Montana State-Northern in its third and final game in the Cactus Classic on a Monday afternoon. According to Coach Welty, Montana State-Northern had one standout player in the scouting report; that was David Harris, and he was surrounded by solid players.

Bryce Davis scored on the opening possession for the Firestorm to give his team an early 2–0 lead. The Stars got off to a strong start and were up 13–8 about eight minutes into the game. Northern maintained the lead at 23–19 with 5:15 before intermission.

Xander Bowers started a 16–0 run to end the first half for ACU by scoring on a dunk to make the score 23–21. The half ended with Paul Hayden hitting a three-pointer right before the horn sounded to put ACU up 35–23. The ACU defense had 11 straight defensive stops during that huge momentum swing.

In the second half, the Firestorm was able to extend its margin to 19 with a 57–38 lead after Gonzalez stole the ball and passed to KeyVaughn Williams for a layup. There was 10:45 left to play.

The feisty Stars were able to avoid the blowout as David Harris scored a game-high 31 points to lead all scorers. Free throws by Wilson, Flowers III, and AJ sealed the nine-point win, 78–69. ACU improved to 14–2, and MS-Northern slipped to 1–4.

ACU had seven players score 8 points or more, with AJ having 14 points and 6 assists. Flowers III and Davis each had 6 rebounds.

"I am proud of our guys! Going 3–0 at the Cactus Classic and doing it against three programs that are frequently at the national tournament is tough to do," Coach Rutter stated after the Monday afternoon game. "We had some great stretches defensively. We had 11 consecutive stops to the end of the half."

This was our last time we would be together as a team before Christmas, so Coach Rutter also prayed for safety for our team, as many guys would be traveling home for several days. The next game would be December 31.

December 31, 2021
PHHacility
Phoenix, Arizona
Park University-Gilbert

After eleven days away from game competition, the ACU Men's Basketball team was set to wrap up play for the calendar year and non-conference schedule. The 14–2

Arizona Christian University Firestorm would face the 4–10 Park University from Gilbert, Arizona.

Park played zone defense the entire game. It took over two minutes for either team to score. Both teams struggled due to being off for Christmas break. AJ opened the scoring with a three-pointer with just under eighteen minutes in the half. Wilson and Flowers III added three-pointers to give the Firestorm a 9–3 lead. AJ and Gonzalez both added three-pointers to give ACU an 18–11 lead with ten minutes left before intermission. The Firestorm continued to maintain the lead throughout the first half by going 8 for 8 from the free throw line, and by getting baskets from Bradford, Davis, Wilson, and AJ. The scoreboard at the PHHacility at halftime read: ACU 38, Park 27. Wilson had 11 points for ACU at the break, while John Norsworthy had 11 for the Buccaneers. Neither team shot the ball very well in the first half, but ACU was 9 of 10 from the free throw line in the half.

Six quick points from Park's big man, Craig Mueller, allowed the Buccaneers to stay in the contest. Mueller scored his eighth point of the half with just over fifteen and a half to play to pull Park within 8 points at 45–37.

A three-pointer by Wilson with just under eleven minutes to play put the Firestorm up 59–43. The Firestorm offense continued to outscore Park down the stretch and expanded the lead to 26 after Dennis Flowers III's layup with 2:37 to play, 78–52.

Two free throws by KeyVaughn Williams, with :36, gave ACU 86 points for the afternoon, while Kyle Short's layup with thirty seconds left in the contest gave Park 64 for the game.

Four players scored in double figures for the game. Wilson led the way with 22 points and 7 boards. Flowers III had 14, AJ 13 and 7 boards, Bowers 10 points and 5 boards. Davis chipped in the 9 and Micah Bradford with 8. The Firestorm made 18 of 22 free throws, 82 percent for the game.

Craig Mueller finished with 17 points and 11 rebounds, 8 offensive, and John Norsworthy had 16 points.

Before leaving the PHHacility, Coach Rutter prayed for our team and reminded the players to make wise choices on this New Year's Eve. We have practice at 10:00 on New Year's Day morning.

CHAPTER 11

JANUARY HIGHS AND LOWS

"There is a time for everything, and a season for every activity under the heavens: A time to be born and a time to die" (Ecclesiastes 3:1–2).

"I have fought the good fight, I have finished the race, I have kept the faith" (2 Tim. 4:7).

January 1, 2022

New Year's Day morning found the Firestorm preparing for the conference games that would restart on Thursday, January 6. It was a practice that involved a lot of team shooting drills and individual skills development.

Coach Rutter also shared a lot of statistical information on where Arizona Christian ranked in different team categories in the GSAC and in the national statistics. It was during this time that Coach V. got a call from his brother to inform him that his father, Henry, passed away that morning at the age of eighty-nine. The news was expected, since Henry had suffered from dementia for years, and he had not been eating or drinking in recent weeks. Thankfully, Coach V. was able to see him one last time when he was back in Wisconsin during Christmas break.

When Coach Rutter was about to wrap up practice, Coach V. broke in with the news. "I'm sorry I had to leave practice for a while. The phone call I just received was from my brother, Larry. He called to let me know that Dad had passed away a few hours ago."

All eyes were on Coach V. by now. Coach V. continued, "Yes, this is sad news, but this is a blessing! Dad had not been in very good health for quite some time. Dad was a follower of Jesus, so we can take comfort to know where he is spending eternity." Coach V. cleared his throat and paused. "I am here at ACU because of him. Dad introduced me to the wonderful game of basketball at a very young age. He took me to my first basketball game many years ago when I was probably four or five years old. We went to our rural Wisconsin high school, Brandon High School, to watch boys from our local church compete."

Paul Hayden and Chris Daniels closed the practice in prayer. Before the guys headed to the locker room, they all took turns to give Coach V. a hug or fist bump and shared their condolences.

Two days later, on January 3, Bryce Davis's maternal grandmother passed away at the age of seventy-two. She also was a Christian, and the team was able to support and pray for Bryce before and after practice. "The passing of my grandma is still one of the most emotionally difficult things I've had to deal with," Davis quietly stated.

Several players and coaches were able to attend her funeral service on January 24.

Bryce's high school coach, Jed Dunn, spoke at the service. Former ACU assistant coach, Josh Cole, gave the main message at the service. Coach Cole got to know the Davis family when he was an assistant with Coach Dunn at Deer Valley High School.

Bryce would be playing with a heavy heart on Thursday, as he would not see his grandmother in the stands for that game. Grandma was a regular attendee at Bryce's games throughout his playing career at Deer Valley High School and at Arizona Christian.

January 6, 2022
The Events Center
Glendale, Arizona
Life Pacific University Warriors
San Dimas, California

Playing in its first game of the New Year and first conference game since December 9, the 15–2 (3–2 GSAC) Firestorm played host to Life Pacific University 4–8 (1–4 GSAC). This game was just days after the deaths of two family members from the ACU team. Coach V. was back in Wisconsin for his father's funeral, and Bryce was playing his first game after the passing of his grandmother. "She was my number-one supporter," Davis stated. "Her favorite hobby was attending my games."

ACU uncharacteristically got off to a roaring start inside the Events Center. Four points from Flowers III, 3 points from AJ, and a basket by Bradford propelled ACU to a 9–0 lead, with the game just two and a half minutes old.

The contest stayed around the ten-point lead range for ACU throughout most of the first half. A Robby Wilson three-pointer and two free throws by Wilson, plus a dunk by Xander Bowers, put the Firestorm up 30–15 with just under seven minutes to the half.

After the dunk by Bowers, Darius Goudeau, "DG," checked into the ACU lineup. Goudeau missed the last five games since he bruised his plantar fascia on December 8. ACU went on a 17-to-11 run to end the half. That included a three-pointer by Darius. The Firestorm shot 52 percent from the floor in the first half and 46 percent from long range to take a 47-to-26 half-time lead.

Arizona Christian maintained that twenty-point margin throughout the early part of the second half. A dunk by Bowers, baskets by AJ and Micah Bradford, and free throws by Bryce Davis expanded the ACU lead to 65–36 with just under twelve minutes left in the game.

Goudeau re-entered the game with just under ten minutes to play, and he made his presence felt. DG went on to score 17 points in the remaining minutes to lead the Firestorm to a 94-to-53 win over Life Pacific.

The win moved the ACU GSAC record to 4–2 and 16–2 overall, while LPU slipped to 1–5 in conference and 4–9 overall.

DG led all scorers with 20 points, going 6 of 11 from deep; Bradford and Flowers III each finished with 11 points. Flowers III added 7 boards. AJ and Davis had 9 points, with AJ adding 6 assists. " I just needed to shut out all the emotions and focus on the task at hand," Davis commented after the game. "I play with the confidence that Grandma is with Jesus and continues to view my games from above." Williams added 5 assists for ACU. Kyler Villarreal led Life Pacific with 14 points.

A very joyful Darius Goudeau was glad to be back out on the floor, helping his team win another game. At one time, Goudeau thought that he may have suffered a season-ending foot injury. "I'm just glad that I am able to contribute any way I can to help this team. It was great to know that teammates were looking for me in the offense. They knew I was back to my previous form and had the hot hand."

January 8, 2022
The Events Center
Glendale, Arizona
Vanguard University Lions
Costa Mesa, California

This Saturday afternoon matinee at the Events Center was a big matchup in the GSAC. ACU entered the contest one game behind Vanguard in the standings. Vanguard was tied, with Hope and William Jessup at 5–1 in the GSAC. ACU needed a win to keep themselves in contention for the top spot in the conference race.

Neither team could take control of the game in the early stages. The score was tied at 14 with 13:32 left in the half.

In the next three minutes, 2 baskets by Bryce Davis, a layup by Williams and a three-pointer by Paul Hayden gave the Firestorm a 23-to-14 advantage. "Playing against Vanguard is a lot of fun," Davis admitted later. They have a competitive program, and a previous college teammate (Jordan Caruso) of mine is on their team." ACU was able to control the final ten minutes of the half with exciting closing seconds. Key Williams connected on 2 free throws to put ACU up 43–29. Then, Dennis Flowers III forced a turnover and was able to hit Bryce Davis, who sprinted down the floor to lay the ball in the hoop as the horn sounded to give the home team a 45–29 lead at the break. There were lots of smiles, cheers, and momentum heading into the locker room.

Four times in the second half, Vanguard was able to battle back and cut the lead to 7 points. The Firestorm offense was up for the challenge and answered and turned away the Lions on all four occasions. AJ nailed a 3 to put ACU up 55–45 with just under fifteen to play. Another three-pointer by Dom Gonzalez gave the Firestorm a 58–48 lead with just thirteen to play. Paul Hayden made a two-point basket with 11:19 left to put ACU up 60–51. Finally, Xander Bowers converted an old-fashioned three-point play to push the lead back to 10, 67–57, with 8:30 still on the clock.

One final push by the Lions cut the deficit to 6, 70–64 with James Moore hitting 2 free throws and over five minutes left to play.

Arizona Christian was able to put the game away with an 18–7 scoring run. Most of those points came from the excellent free-throw shooting, 11–12, with AJ going 6–6. Final score was 88–71.

"Fellas, we turned the ball only 9 times," Coach Jeff Rutter commented. "We stood up and turned away many comeback attempts by Vanguard, and we were 11–12 from the free throw line in the closing minutes. That is what good teams do!"

Four of the starters for ACU were in double figures, and Micah Bradford had 8.

AJ led the way with 15, Flowers III with 14, Davis 13 points and 9 boards, and Wilson 11 points and 6 boards. Off the bench, Bowers had 10 points, while Williams had 7 points and 5 assists.

Vanguard's Chris Wilson led all scorers with 18 points. "Credit ACU for having great focus and execution at home," said Coach Rhett Soliday. "They played a really good first half, and that was the difference in the game."

ACU improved to 5–2 in GSAC and 17–2 overall. Vanguard slipped to 5–2 and 12–5. Next weekend, the Firestorm will be on the road in the San Francisco area for two more difficult games.

January 13, 2022
Haynes-Prim Pavilion
Menlo College Oaks
Atherton, California

This Thursday night matchup had the NAIA's eighth-ranked team in the country, riding an eight-game winning streak playing at the Menlo Oaks. A team that received votes in the last poll, ACU was 16–3 overall and 5–2 in the GSAC, while Menlo was 12–4 and 4–3.

On the drive from ACU's hotel to the Menlo campus, the team traveled past Stanford University in Palo Alto.

Menlo would start the game, with their two top guards out for medical reasons. So, the Oaks would be without Khalid Price, who averages 7 points per game, and N'jai LeBlanc, who averaged 15 points per game. The loss of two starters did not phase the Oaks as they came out of the gates inspired. Harrison Bonner was forced to handle some of the ball-handling duties because of the lack of guards available for this game.

Menlo's 6'7" Parker Haven connected on his first two jumpers one minute into the game to give the home team a 4–0 lead. Bryce Davis and Micah Bradford answered with a layup and a three-pointer to put ACU up 5–4 at the sixteen-minute mark. The game seesawed back and forth for the next few minutes of play.

A three-pointer by Haven and two baskets in the lane by Corey Le'Aupepe and a three-pointer by Adam Orr stretched the Menlo lead to 22–12, with just over nine minutes left before intermission. Menlo stretched the lead to 14 points before ACU trimmed the lead to 8 on a layup by AJ, with under thirty seconds before the break.

The halftime score was 32 to 24; Menlo on top and ACU scoring its lowest points in a half for the season. ACU did not play with a sense of urgency and shot the ball poorly, shooting 35 percent for the floor and 2 for 13 from long range. Also Bryce Davis was limited with playing time because of foul trouble. Mento shot 48 percent from the floor and 4 of 10 from deep.

At halftime, Coach Rutter stressed the importance of pressuring the Oaks more in the full court. "Menlo's two starting guards are not playing; we need to tire out their guards and get them out of their comfort zones. We failed to do that in the first half."

Just like the start of the game, Parker Haven made a basket just seconds into the half to put the Oaks up 34–24. ACU went on an 18-to-6 run, with Flowers III contributing 10 points. Davis made a layup with 13:41 to cut the deficit to 2 (42–40).

Menlo was able to build a 47–40 lead, but three-pointers from Marcus Green and Key Williams, and layups by Williams and Paul Hayden, pulled the Firestorm back to even at 50 with just over ten minutes left in the game.

Menlo's Jake Tranter was able to hit back-to-back three pointers to put the Oaks back in front; ACU responded with a comeback.

It was finished off with 3 points from Bowers and a layup by Williams to give the lead back to the Firestorm for the first time since early in the contest; ACU 59 and Menlo 58 with just under six minutes left. Here we go, again, with another nip-and tuck-battle.

The ACU lead was expanded to 5 with layups from AJ and Robby Wilson, with just under five minutes to play. Tranter hit another 3 for Menlo, and Flowers III made a layup to make the score 65–61 ACU, with 1:43 left.

Patrick Ryan of Menlo and AJ both made one of two free throws to keep it at a four-point game 66–64 with :25 left to play. Parker Haven was fouled with :14 seconds left, and Haven made both free throws to cut the lead to 2, 66–64. No time-out was called, but many substitutions were made at this point, ACU loading up with better offensive players, and Menlo putting its best defensive squad out on the floor.

With nine ticks left on the clock, Harrison Bonner fouled AJ who is a 78 percent-free-throw shooter on the year. He had been in this position many times before in his career. Surprisingly, AJ missed the front end of the bonus free throws, and Le'Aupepe grabbed the rebound and called time-out. Again, many offense-for-defense and defense-for-offense substitutions were made by both teams during the time-out. Menlo could either go for the tie or the win with a three-pointer, having the full 94 feet to go.

Inside the ACU huddle, "Make sure to switch on all screens," Coach Rutter stated calmly. "Stay in front of your man, contest any shot without fouling, and we must box out and not allow an offensive putback by Menlo."

The basketball was inbounded to Adam Orr, and he quickly dribbled up the left sideline. Orr ran a dribble handoff to Harrison Bonner on the sideline, right in front of the Menlo bench. Bonner took the handoff, took two dribbles toward the middle of the floor, and launched a long three-pointer, just clearing the long, outstretched hand of Bowers. The ball arched high, toward the rafters. It was one of those shots that seemed to put life into slow motion. When the ball finally came down, it swished through the net as the horn sounded, and the scoreboard read: Menlo 67 ACU 66. The Menlo benched cleared and went storming on the floor in jubilation, looking for Bonner. He had sprinted to the far corner in his celebration run. To borrow a line from sportscaster Jim McKay from the old ABC Wide World of Sports program, "The thrill of victory and the agony of defeat!" It was one of those shots that Bonner would make one time out of twenty-five tries. That is what makes sports so intriguing to watch. The unpredictability of some of the outcomes keeps spectators watching and coming to games.

The ACU players walked quietly and in a daze to go through the handshake line with the Menlo players and coaches. The players and coaches returned to the bench to retrieve warmup tops, clipboards, and so on, and slowly made their way to the locker room. A tough loss like this brings an awkward silence in the locker room. There is a pang in the stomach, and the head is just buzzing with so many thoughts. It is such a shock to the whole body. No one says anything because all of this is going on with our bodies.

As the coaches assembled into the locker room, most of the players were just staring at the floor. Coach Rutter just stood in front of the team for what seemed like minutes before saying anything. "This loss is hard to take. We need to learn from it. We waited until the second half, when we were 14 points down, before we played with a sense of urgency. We need to bounce back because Saturday's game at William Jessup will be a battle. Let's pray."

For the game, Menlo shot 51 percent from the floor, 47 percent from long range, and 7 for 8, 87 percent from the free throw line. ACU shot 50 percent from the floor, 33 percent from three-point range, and only 5 for 11, 45 percent from the line.

"This was a difficult team to prepare for," Coach Oetjen commented after the game. "Coach Rooney did a great job in disguising the offensive actions and layering them, so it was tough to know when they were going."

Menlo was led by Parker Haven with 14 points, shooting 5–8, grabbing 4 rebounds, and dishing out 4 assists. Le'aupepe had 12 points, 5 boards, and 7 assists. Tranter, Ryan, and Orr combined to score 28 points, filling in for LeBlanc and Price, who were not medically cleared to play in the game. Bonner finished with the game-winning shot, 9 points, and 9 assists in thirty-six minutes of play.

Dennis Flowers III led all scorers with 19 for ACU. "We learned a valuable lesson in this loss," Flowers III admitted. "Little details and timing matter. We switched on the game-winning shot, but we did it too slowly."

AJ had 11 points, 7 rebounds, and 3 assists. Wilson had 10 and 8. Davis was held to 4 points on 2 of 2 from the floor, with limited playing time because of foul trouble.

Again, Williams inspired the Firestorm in the second half. "I think our players were a little over-confident with Menlo's two guards out of the lineup. We got out to a slow start; I just wanted to give us a lift. I was able to create some space and get to the hoop for baskets." Williams was 4 of 4 from the floor, with 9 points and 2 assists in eighteen minutes of playing time.

Hours after the game, Coach Rutter had this to say about the loss: "Tonight is on me. I did not have us ready to go from the start. Give credit to Menlo; they executed their game plan and had guys step up and make big shots. It wasn't until we were down 14 before we started to play with a sense of urgency. We played a good second half, but we just got off to such a bad start. I'm proud of how the guys battled back and gave us a chance to win."

January 15, 2022
Warrior Arena
William Jessup University Warriors
Rocklin, California

The GSAC game of the week was between the fourth-ranked team and first-place William Jessup at 7–1 GSAC and 19–1 overall versus the eighth-ranked team and third-place team in the league at 5–3 and 17–3 overall. This matchup was switched to a noon start time to allow ACU to make their late-afternoon flight back to Phoenix.

Both teams struggled to score early on. ACU took an 8–1 lead three minutes into the game, with points coming from three free throws from Flowers III and three-pointers by Wilson and a layup for Bradford. WJU was able to cut the deficit to 4 at 18–14, with twelve minutes left.

The Firestorm then went on a 10–0 run, with the last four points coming from Marcus Green. ACU was up 28–14, with 8:23 before halftime.

The Warriors then went on a 12-to-2 scoring run by hitting 4 three-pointers, with two of those coming from Corey Myles. With just under six minutes left, ACU was up 30–26. WJU cut the lead to 2 with a minute left before half at 37–35.

In the last :30 of the half, Marcus Green scored on a dunk off of a steal by Davis and an assist from Flowers III. Green then stole the inbound pass, made a layup, and made the free throw after being fouled on the play. The quick five-point scoring burst from Marcus gave ACU a 42–35 halftime lead. "The lift Marcus gave right before half was huge," Coach Welty boasted. Momentum was with the Firestorm, heading into the second half.

The two leading scorers at the half were Paul Hayden with 11 and Marcus Green with 9. "This was a must-win for us to stay in the conference race," Hayden observed later on. "The players stepped up for the challenge." The two top scorers for WJU for the season both had 8 points at the half.

The team half-time statistics were very even, with both teams shooting around 50 percent from the floor.

The Firestorm continued to score as the second half started. Davis hit 2 free throws twelve seconds into the half. That was followed up by Wilson and AJ making baskets to push the lead to 10 at 48–38 two minutes into the half.

The Warriors responded with a 9–2 run of their own to pull within 1 at 50–49 with Tim Strijaous's layup, with just under twelve minutes to play. ACU would not be outdone, so the Firestorm returned the favor and went on a 9–2 run. Baskets came from AJ and Bradford, and 5 points came from Davis, 59–51 ACU, with 8:43 to play.

With 4:04 left, Micah Bradford nailed a three-pointer from the left corner to put the Firestorm up 68–60. Bradford made another layup with two minutes left to put the Firestorm up 73–64.

The Warriors' Cash Williams made a layup, Myles Corey had a dunk, and Tim

Strijaous made 2 free throws to cut the deficit to 3 at 73–70. There were now forty-four seconds left in the contest. Bradford and AJ went 1 of 2 from the line to give the Firestorm a five-point cushion, with twenty-four ticks left.

Cash Williams went 1 of 2 for WJU, and Wilson went 1 of 2 for ACU with :16 and a 76–71 lead. WJU came down the floor with Jayden DeJoseph nailing a three-pointer and making it a two-point lead, ACU 76–74.

AJ was fouled with six seconds left, and the junior point guard made both free throws to ice the game for the Firestorm. Cash Williams was fouled with two seconds left, and he made the first free throw to cut it to a three-point lead. On the second attempt, Williams intentionally missed the second attempt, hoping for an offensive rebound and a quick three. Xander Bowers was able to dash those hopes as he corralled the rebound when the final horn sounded.

ACU led from wire to wire and knocked off the fourth-ranked team in the country,

78–75. It was the second top-ten win for the Firestorm of the season. In December, ACU beat second-ranked Carroll of Montana.

The loss left Hope International alone in first place at 8–1, WJU in second place at 7–2, and ACU in third place at 6–3.

What a different feeling from two nights ago. Coach Rutter was pleased how his team was able to bounce back after a tough loss. "We did a great job defensively and executed well. It was great to have another opportunity to close a game out on the road after Thursday night at Menlo when we did not finish as well."

Coach Oetjen echoed those thoughts: "This was a big-time win on the road! It is tough to win after a letdown loss. Our guys handled it with poise and relentless grit."

From the free throw line, ACU was 19–28 for 68 percent, while the Warriors were 14–24, 58 percent. Most of the other stats were very even, and ACU did record 13 steals.

Four ACU players scored in double figures. Micah Bradford led the way with 14 points on 5-of-8 shooting, Hayden with 13, AJ 12, Davis 11 and 7 boards. Marcus Green had 9 big points in the first half, while Wilson had 8. Bowers and Flowers III both had 6 boards.

Warriors' Head Coach Lance Von Vogt responded after the hard-fought battle, "Give them (ACU) all the credit for doing what it took to make the plays throughout the game and down the stretch to win." William Jessup had four players with double digits. Cash Williams with 19, Myles Corey with 12, DeJoseph 11, and Tim Strijaous had 10 points and 7 rebounds coming off the bench.

Some added good news for the afternoon: the team was able to drop off the rental vans and get to the Sacramento airport in time to make the flight back to Phoenix.

January 20, 2022
MacArthur Center
The Master's University Mustangs
Santa Clarita, California

The second round of the GSAC schedule started with ACU traveling to California for the second week in a row. The Firestorm is in third place in the league standings at 6–3, trailing behind first-place Hope and second-place William Jessup. The Firestorm needed to keep winning games to maintain any chance to stay in the conference championship race.

Again, the Firestorm was playing in the game of the week with a matchup in Santa Clarita, California, against The Master's University. In the first matchup of the season, the Firestorm held the Mustangs to 57 points and forced 24 turnovers. That will be a tough task to repeat on the road.

The contest got off to a promising start for the Mustangs, who took an early 6–0 lead off of Jordan Starr's two three-pointers.

The game was just over three minutes old before Bryce Davis scored the first basket for ACU. The Master's held an 8–5 lead with just over sixteen minutes to play in the half.

The Firestorm then went on a 12–0 run in the next six minutes, capped off by a three-pointer by Dom Gonzalez off of a pass from Key Williams. Williams who would end up with 6 helpers on the night. The new score now was 17 to 8, ACU.

Scoring from Caleb Lowery and Jordan Starr kept the Mustangs in the game. Some late-half scoring from Flowers III, Wilson, and Johnson gave the Firestorm a 33-to-26 halftime lead.

In the second half, Starr hit a basket early to cut the lead to 5, but behind the scoring from Davis and Flowers III, ACU took a 39–28 lead with just over seventeen minutes to play.

The ACU lead stayed around 10 points for the next ten minutes until back-to-back layups from Davis and Flowers III pushed the lead to 14 points with just over seven and a half minutes to play.

The Firestorm was able to take its biggest lead of the night after a layup by Flowers III and a dunk by Bowers at 2:46 with the score of 61–43. ACU was able to match baskets with the Mustangs and took a 67–53 GSAC win.

The stingy ACU defense only allowed 53 points to the Mustangs, forced 20 turnovers, and held them to 37 percent shooting from the floor. Starr ended up with 17 points for TMU and Lowery had 12. "I felt like we controlled the tempo for much of the game and played good defense. We just could not score," Master's Head Coach Kelvin Starr commented after the game. "You can't beat a team that good if you can't put the ball in the hoop."

Dennis Flowers III was 8 of 10 from the floor and led all scorers with 19 points and 5 rebounds and 2 steals. "This was one of those games where I played with so much confidence and freedom," Flowers III shared after the game. Davis had 10 points and 5 boards.

Bowers had a productive game on both ends with 10 points, 4 rebounds, 1 block, and 1 assist. Wilson had 6 rebounds and Williams had 6 assists.

One down and one to go on the road trip. Coach Rutter shared with the team in the locker room that William Jessup beat Hope by two points. So, that leaves those two teams with two losses each and ACU with three losses. The GSAC title chase just got closer.

Also on Thursday, the GSAC office announced that due to the oddity of the season with COVID issues, all basketball teams will make the GSAC postseason men's tournament hosted by Hope International in Fullerton, California. Normally the top six teams make the GSAC conference tournament.

January 21, 2022
Travel Day to Westmont

The team left Santa Clarita Friday morning after breakfast. Coach Rutter had arranged for us to stop at Oxnard High School on the drive. Years ago, Coach Jeff Staniland, the boys' head coach at Oxnard, played for Coach Rutter at Azusa Pacific. Coach Staniland had reserved one of their gyms for our team to get a shooting workout in. It pays to have connections, and Coach Rutter certainly has his fair share throughout the country.

Since some players would rather sleep in than eat breakfast, we stopped at a shopping center that offered many different meal options. Also, Darius Goudeau, the snappy dresser on the team, made time to pick up a few clothing items at Nordstrom.

It is quite a treat to drive up the 101 from Oxnard to the Santa Barbara area during the afternoon. The Pacific Ocean is on the left side of the road, and the small mountain range is on the right. The big, orange ball in the sky glistens off the ocean. On January 21, the only thing the sun glistens off of in the Midwest is the snow. Both scenes make us appreciate the beauty of God's creation.

It was a short half-mile walk from the Best Western Hotel in Carpinteria, where the team was spending the night, to the ocean beach. Most of the coaching staff and most of the players found their way down to the beach. Coach O., of course, was the only brave soul to get fully wet. Most of us just walked the beach and waded ankle-deep in the chilly waters of the Pacific.

That evening, the team dinner was at Giovanni's Italian restaurant. We had some gym time at Westmont College at 7:00 p.m. The team got shots up and got familiar with the facility for Saturday's game.

January 22, 2022
Murchison Gym
Westmont College Warriors
Santa Barbara, California

The last time the Firestorm played at Murchison Gymnasium was back in March of 2020. That is the day ACU used a last-second side-out-of-bounds play to win the GSAC conference championship tournament game, which earned them an automatic bid to the NAIA national tournament. Unfortunately, they never got to play in the tournament because it was canceled due to COVID-19.

Motivation was not an issue for the Firestorm on this Saturday afternoon. Westmont defeated the Firestorm 82–80 in early December. ACU also needed to keep winning games to stay in the conference race. "When we played at Westmont," Xander Bowers recalled, "I knew I owed them one. Some of their players had some choice words for me when we lost to them in December. I just had winning on my mind."

It did not take long for the home team to get off to a good start. In the first minute of the game, Jared Brown hit a jumper and 2 free throws by Jalen Townsell, giving the Warriors the early 4–0 lead.

The Firestorm then went on a 20–2 run with points coming from five different players. The scoring run was capped off by a three-point basket by AJ. ACU was up 20–6 with 13:44 to play before half.

Westmont responded with a 34–14 offensive run to end the half. Fourteen of Westmont's points came from freshman left-hand-shooting Nate Meithof. The home team regained the lead and took a 40–34 advantage in the locker room.

ACU ran a set play to open the second half, which ended with AJ scoring a layup and cut the lead to 4 points. After cutting the lead to 4, Westmont slowly built a double-digit lead. After Meithof hit 3 free throws, the Warriors led by 12 at 60–48 with just over thirteen minutes left in this GASC matchup.

Senior Xander Bowers and Paul Hayden started the Firestorm comeback with a basket and three-pointer, respectively. Micah Bradford's three-pointer at the 10:10 mark cut the deficit to 7 points at 65–58.

Two free throws by ACU's KeyVaughn Williams at 7:19 cut the lead to 68–63. A layup and free throw by Dennis Flowers III pulled the Firestorm to within 3 points at 72–69 with 5:47 to go.

Westmont got a basket from Cly Griffith Jr. to lead by 5 a minute later. A basket from Bowers and a free throw from Davis pulled the Firestorm to within 2 at 74–72 with just over three and a half minutes left.

Westmont's Jared Brown answered quickly with a three-pointer to give the home team a five-point lead. Looks like the Firestorm was in for another thriller.

AJ made 2 free throws, and Williams added another free throw to pull the Firestorm to within 2 at 77–75 with 2:43 left.

Jalen Townsell connected on 2 free throws to give Westmont a four-point lead at 79–74.

AJ then scored 5 straight points on a layup and 3 free throws. This gave ACU its first lead in the second half, 80–79, with forty-seven ticks left on the clock.

With twenty seconds left, Griffith made one of two free throws to knot the score up at 80–all. Coach Rutter called a time-out.

Once again, the Firestorm players in the huddle were confident that they would get a good look for a go-ahead shot, and the chance to pull out another victory in a hard-fought battle. Having AJ with the ball in his hands would give anyone confidence to make something good happen. Just like in previous close games, AJ ended up with the orange sphere in his hands with ten seconds left on the clock. With four seconds left, AJ drove left with lightning speed, and beat the 6'5" Meithof to the rim. AJ laid in the ball high off the glass for the go-ahead basket with 1.2 seconds left on the clock with ACU up 82–80.

"This time," AJ recalled, "I was trying to draw a foul on the play. I had a much taller player on me, so I had to shoot the ball really high."

Westmont used a time-out to set up a play to catch and shoot to either win or tie the game. Westmont's Townsell attempted to throw a long pass, but it was tipped at half-court by ACU, and the final buzzer sounded with no shot attempt. The comeback was complete 82–80—the exact same score that Westmont beat ACU with back in December in Glendale, Arizona.

The big come-from-behind victory was a special birthday present for Head Coach Rutter and Assistant Coach Jackson Oldham.

"Great win today! I am really impressed with the resolve of this team," Coach Rutter complimented his team after the win. "This caps off four brutal road games in a row. To win three of four is big-time.

"We got off to a good start, but we gambled after that, and it led to foul trouble. Westmont has some talented offensive players, and we played a long stretch without some of our best defenders. We needed to be a little more aggressive in the second half, and we hung around. AJ did what he does at the end of the game. I am really proud of our guys," Coach Rutter concluded.

Westmont was 29–34, 85 percent from the free throw line. ACU was 15–18, 83 percent from the stripe. ACU shot better from the floor than Westmont, 48 percent to 37 percent; three-point land ACU 7–26 27 percent to WC 9–26, 35 percent.

Nate Meithof led all scorers with 30 points. Cly Griffith Jr. came off the bench to score 24 points, playing heavy minutes with Roth out with a broken collar bone. Jared Brown had 12 points, and Jalen Townsell led the team with 9 boards.

Four players scored in double figures for ACU. AJ led the way with a game-winner and 26 points, Flowers III with 16, and Davis with 11. AJ, Davis, and Robby Wilson all had 6 rebounds on the afternoon. Bowers finished with 15 points and 5 rebounds on the day. Eleven of the points came in the second half. He was 6 of 8 from the floor and 3 of 3 from the line. Bowers also played solid defense for the Firestorm.

"This was the best half Xander has played all year long," Coach V. observed. " Xander had an ankle injury early in the season that bothered him, and then there was a chance he would redshirt, so he sat out some games. This was a breakout game for Xander. We need him to play like this if we want to meet our team goals for the season."

It was a happy locker room as players celebrated the big win. Surprisingly, the first words out of Coach Rutter's mouth was about football and not about the game. "Please don't say anything about the Cincinnati Bengals game!" Coach spent his early childhood life in Ohio, and he continues to support the Bengals. The Bengals played the Tennessee Titans in the AFC playoffs that day. Coach Oldham was going to drive one of the vans back to Arizona, with Coach Rutter riding shotgun. That way, Coach

Rutter could watch his beloved Bengals and enjoy his large Diet Coke on the six-hour drive back. It was quite a special birthday for Coach with the Bengals upsetting the Titans and the Firestorm getting the big road win.

CHAPTER 12

FIRESTORM
KEEPS ROLLING

"But those who hope in the Lord will renew their strength. They will soar on wings like eagles; they will run and not grow weary; they will walk and not faint" (Isaiah 40:31).

January 27, 2022
The Events Center
Glendale, Arizona
San Diego Christian Hawks

After being on the road in California the past two weekends, it was refreshing to be playing at home in the Events Center for the next two games. By winning three of four on the road, they kept the Firestorm in the GSAC conference title race at 8 and 3.

The opponent for this Thursday night matchup was the Hawks from San Diego Christian University. This is a team that ACU struggled to beat on the road in November.

ACU got off to a solid start with baskets by AJ, Flowers III, and a three-pointer by Robby Wilson. ACU was up 7–2 three and a half minutes into the game. The Firestorm kept the early momentum going with 2 more hoops from AJ and 2 baskets by Bowers, including a tip-in at the 13:31 mark, putting the Firestorm up 17–4.

The Hawks were able to trim the lead to 7 points at 21–14 when Kyle Ruiz hit a three-pointer with just over eleven minutes left to play in the half.

ACU answered the comeback with a 13–0 run in the next three and a half minutes to take a twenty-point lead at 34–14. Paul Hayden, Bryce Davis, KeyVaughn Williams, and Flowers III each scored a basket, while Marcus Green added a three-pointer and 2 free throws in the scoring barrage.

The lead stayed around 20 points until the last minute of the half, when Hayden hit 2 free throws and a jumper with four seconds left to give the Firestorm a 52–28 halftime lead. ACU shot a blistering 67 percent in the first half and held a 21–8 advantage with rebounds.

The second half started for ACU the way the first half ended. Three-pointers by Micah Bradford and Wilson, and a layup by AJ, and 5 free throws from Flowers III, expanded the lead to 65–32 with sixteen minutes left to play.

The next six minutes of play saw the Firestorm bulge the lead to 39 points at 79–40 after Darius Goudeau hit a jumper.

Josh O'Campo hit several big threes in the second half for the Hawks to bring the score to 90–50 with four and a half minutes left.

Playing in his first game for ACU since pulling a ligament on his left-hand ring finger in November, Pat Fisher assisted on back-to-back dunks by Marcus Green, cutting to the basket down the right baseline. The two dunks stretched the lead to 94–50. Green added another three-pointer, and Chris Daniels scored with twenty-six seconds left that gave the Firestorm a 99–60 win over San Diego Christian.

After the team assembled in the locker room, Coach Rutter announced to the team that Ottawa University knocked off Hope International. The win by ACU, and the loss by Hope, tied the teams for second place in the GSAC. Both teams were one game behind William Jessup University. Hope and ACU would play for sole possession of second place on Saturday afternoon at the Events Center.

All the players for ACU scored in the contest. Six players were in double digits, with Freshman Marcus Green leading the way with a career-high 16 points. Green went

6 for 6 from the floor and 2 for 2 from the line. Wilson added 14, Bowers and Flowers III had 11 each, and AJ and Hayden each had 10 points. Shaun Wahlstrom hauled in a team-best 9 rebounds. O'Campo led all scorers with 26 for the Hawks.

ACU improved to 9 and 3 in the GSAC and 21–3 overall, while San Diego Christian slipped to 3–8 and 12–8 overall.

January 29, 2022
The Events Center
Glendale, Arizona
Hope International Royals

This Saturday matinee GSAC matchup was between eighth-ranked ACU and seventeenth-ranked Hope and for sole possession of second place in the conference. Hope was coming off a Thursday night loss at Ottawa University just twenty minutes down the road from ACU, while the Firestorm was coming off a win over San Diego Christian. ACU was also trying to even the season series with the Royals after losing by 16 points in November—a game in which the Firestorm struggled on both ends of the floor.

Playing in front of the largest crowd of the season at home, the Firestorm would be facing a Hope team that would start the game without their starting-five man, Josh Powell-Davis. Powell-Davis was injured in practice the day before.

The Royals won the tip and scored 26 seconds later on a jumper by Sebastian Castro. Micah Bradford answered with a three-pointer from the left corner to put ACU up 3–2 one minute into the game.

The Royals regained the lead shortly after that. With 14:36 left in the half, Paul Hayden hit a three-pointer followed by a dunk by Bryce Davis and a jumper by Davis to put ACU back in front at 13–10.

Three-pointers by AJ and Bradford and two-pointers by Wilson and Davis put the Firestorm up 23–17, with just under seven minutes before halftime.

ACU extended the first half lead after a three-pointer by Flowers III and a layup by Wilson. With 4:26 left in the half from the top of the key, Dom Gonzalez drilled his first three-pointer of the afternoon and a 31–18 Firestorm lead.

Powell-Davis entered the game for the Royals late in the first half. With 1:15 before intermission, Powell Davis scored a layup followed up by a Rasheet Wilson layup for Hope and a basket by Anthony Garcia, with one second left before the half, to pull the visitors to within 2 points at 36–34. ACU had the lead, but Hope had the momentum going into the halftime break.

Coach Rutter's message at the half was to keep up the stifling defense on their great shooters and to cut down on the turnovers. ACU committed 12 turnovers in the first half.

On ACU's second possession of the second half, AJ connected from long range, giving the home team a 39–34 lead. The Royals then answered with a basket by Powell-Davis and a tip-in by Sebastian

Castro to make it a one-point ACU lead, 39–38, with just over eighteen minutes to play.

Hope was able to tie the score at 46–all when Castro connected on 2 free throws with 13:13 to play. ACU's Dom Gonzalez hit his second three of the day, off of an assist from Bryce Davis, to put ACU up 49–46. Charles Neal answered for Hope with a deep three to tie the score at 49.

Gonzalez then hit two more threes in the next thirty seconds to put the Firestorm up 55–49, with 11:28 left, and forced Hope to call a time-out to slow down the momentum. After the game, Dom commented, "The moment is not too big. Basketball is 70 percent mental and 30 percent physical. Staying neutral is what I do in games, sort of like Kawhi Leonard and Tim Duncan." Free throws by Wilson and Williams gave ACU a ten-point lead at 59–49 with 9:10 in the game.

The Firestorm kept building the lead with a three-point play by Davis, a three-pointer by Bradford, and a jumper by AJ to push the score to 67–52. Another time-out was used by Hope as the game was getting into the danger zone for the Royals.

After the time-out, Hope responded with 4 free throws to cut the lead to 68–56, with six minutes left, to determine what team would take over sole possession of second place in the league. ACU answered with 2 dunks by Bowers, a layup by Williams, and a free throw by AJ. This stretched the lead to 19 points at 75–56 with just over four minutes to play.

Brandon Thomas hit a three-pointer with under a minute left for Hope to cut the lead to 14 at 78–64. Micah Bradford capped off his best offensive game of the season as he hit a hanging jumper with twenty-six seconds left. The final score was ACU 80, Hope 64.

"This was a great game just to see how much we improved since we played in November," Coach Rutter commented after the game. We are a different team. Our guys are well-prepared by knowing the scouting report, and we did a great job executing defensively today. Micah and AJ did a nice job in defending Hope's big shooters. Dom came in and gave us a big lift by hitting those threes that opened up the game."

ACU shot 52 percent on the afternoon, which included 44 percent from long range. Hope shot 40 percent and 25 percent. The Firestorm out-rebounded the Royals 39 to 25. Hope turned the ball over 10 times, while ACU had 18 with only 6 in the second half.

Once again, there was a balanced scoring attack by the Firestorm with Bradford scoring 16 points and 6 rebounds. Gonzalez had 12 points from 4 three-pointers. Wilson had 11 points and 5 boards. AJ had 10 points and 4 assists. Davis had 10 points and 6 boards. Bowers, Williams, and Flowers III each finished with 6 points, with Bowers hauling in 6 rebounds. Bowers also had 2 dunks that halted a comeback by Hope.

The win moved ACU into second place in the GSAC at 10–3, while Hope dropped to 9–4 and third place in the league.

The Firestorm will venture out to California for its final road trip of the regular season, with games at Vanguard and Life Pacific.

February 3, 2022
The Pit
Vanguard University Lions
Costa Mesa, California

Having defeated Hope International last weekend, the Firestorm hit the road for its final regular-season road trip of the season. It was another trip to the Golden State, the third trip in four weeks. The trip to California on I-10 west was an adventure on the Wednesday travel day. The caravan of vans traveled through a good-old Southwestern desert sandstorm. "The storm was so intense," Coach V. remembered. "It would hit for thirty seconds, and then it would be clear for a while. There would be debris and large objects flying around. In addition, there was a lot of traffic, including eighteen-wheelers." Most of the ACU coaches experienced driving through snow whiteouts in the Midwest, but this was the first time driving through a sandstorm. Thankfully, everyone made it to our destination safely.

Thursday night's matchup was between the second-place ACU Firestorm at 10–3 against fourth-place Vanguard Lions at 7–5. The game was played at the Pit on the Vanguard University campus in Costa Mesa, California.

Vanguard wasted little time taking the early lead when Phillip Willis scored a jumper twelve seconds into the contest. The Firestorm responded with a 9–0 run to take a 9–2 lead with sixteen minutes left in the half.

Vanguard answered with a 9–2 run of their own when Isaac Davis tied the score at 11, with just under thirteen to play in the half.

ACU's Paul Hayden hit back-to-back jumpers to give the lead back to the Firestorm at 15–11. "Looking back at this contest," Hayden later stated, "this was my best game of the year." It was a lead that they would not give up for the rest of the game. Two three-pointers by Wilson and one three-pointer by Bowers, and a nice backdoor cut with a dunk by Hayden assisted by Williams put the Firestorm up 10 at 32–22, with three and a half minutes before the break. "Everything was clicking for us at this time. It seemed like practice," Hayden added.

Four points by Vanguard's Garrett White cut the lead to 32–28 with ninety seconds left in the half. Then, a three-pointer by Hayden and 2 free throws from Bowers put the Firestorm out in front, 37–28 at halftime.

Robby Wilson of the Firestorm kept his hot shooting going as he connected from long range fifteen seconds into the second half, 40–28. ACU was able to stretch the lead to 15 with free throws from Wilson, 2 layups from Bowers, and layups from Williams and

Hayden to push the score to 53–38 with just over fourteen minutes to play.

Dom Gonzalez was able to help extend the lead to 20 points by hitting a three-point basket and 2 free throws, 74–54 with 5:45 on the clock.

The Lions fought back to slice into the deficit, and at the 1:46 mark, they got a three-pointer from Jon Scherer. This made it a twelve-point game at 79–67. Layups by Williams and Bowers, and free throws by AJ, gave the Firestorm an 85–70 win over the Vanguard Lions.

Going into the game, Coach Welty had on the scouting report that Vanguard had been playing well at home and shooting so much better in The Pit.

It turned out, in this game, that ACU had the hot-shooting touch. ACU shot 56 percent from the floor, 42 percent from long range, and 15–18 from the line for 83 percent. Meanwhile, Vanguard shot 39 percent from the floor, 35 percent from deep, and

13–17 (77 percent) from the line. ACU won the battle on the boards, 32 to 23.

The stingy ACU defense was able to hold the five Vanguard starters to 17 points, but the Lions got 53 bench points, with White leading the way with 20. This was one time the ACU bench got outscored in a game. ACU's bench points totaled 42.

"Every time we made a push and had a chance to get within striking distance, they made a defensive stop or a big shot," observed Vanguard Coach Rhett Soliday. "That is why they are one of the top teams in the country."

Robby Wilson led the Firestorm with 19 points going 4–8 from long range. Three other teammates scored in double digits with AJ's 15; Bowers and Hayden were both 6 of 7 from the field. Bowers finished with 15 points and 8 boards. Hayden ended the night with 14. Gonzalez had 7 points going 2 for 2 from the floor and 2 for 2 from the line. Williams had 6 points and 4 helpers.

February 5, 2022
Mehl Court
Life Pacific University Warriors
San Dimas, California

After coming off another big win in a difficult place to win on Thursday at Vanguard, the Firestorm was ready to close out another California GSAC road trip at Life Pacific University in San Dimas.

In early January, ACU clobbered LPU by 40 points, so the theme for the scouting report, prepared by Coach Oetjen, was "be mentally tough." Coach O. also had the team read different scriptures which dealt with humility. "God opposes the proud, but shows favor to the humble" (James 4:6). "Humble yourselves before the Lord, and He will lift you up" (James 4:10). Coach also stressed the importance of not looking at past scores and stressing that the Warriors were playing tough in the conference. As any coach of any sport will tell you, one of the toughest jobs of coaching is to motivate a team that thinks they can win by just showing up.

Coach Rutter was also concerned how the team practiced on Friday. Most coaches also know a team plays like it practices. When it comes to the game, a coach can say all the right things to motivate and prepare the players, but the players play the game. This lack of motivation or over-confidence happens at all levels; it is human nature.

ACU scored the first basket when Robby Wilson hit a three-pointer a minute into the game. Give Life Pacific a ton of credit, because the Warriors came out determined to give the Firestorm a game. LPU went on a 14–4 run capped-off by a three-point basket by Austin Cook. That gave LPU a 14–7 lead with twelve and a half minutes left before halftime.

The Firestorm responded to the Warriors' run with a 13–0 run of their own. That run included three-pointers from Gonzalez and Bowers; layups from Hayden, AJ, and Green;

and a free throw from Davis. With 9:14 left in the half, ACU took a 20–14 lead.

For the rest of the half, the teams exchanged baskets, but LPU gained some momentum heading into the locker room when Pedro Leal-Cruz hit a long three as the horn sounded, ending the first half. ACU was left hanging onto a 38–35 lead.

The halftime statistics were pretty even for the teams. Austin Cook from LPU led all scorers with 12 points, while Robby Wilson had 7 for the Firestorm. ACU also only had 2 turnovers at the break. Life had 17 rebounds to ACU's 13. Coach Rutter's message at the half was simple: "We warned you guys that Life would play us hard at home. We need to be prepared for more of the same in the second half. Be patient on offense, and try to make the extra pass. Starters, we need you to step up and lead this team in the second half!"

The Warriors' Leal-Cruz started the second half by connecting from long range to tie the score at 38. The next six minutes saw the teams exchange leads and tied scores.

With 13:07, Life was up 51–48. The Warriors were giving everything to give the second-place Firestorm all they could handle.

Robby Wilson put back an offensive rebound at 8:41 to give the lead back to the Firestorm at 62–61, a lead that they would hold onto for the rest of the day. In the game, there were 12 lead changes and 4 ties.

After the putback by Wilson, ACU went on a 13–4 run. During that run, the Firestorm got three-pointers from AJ, Williams, and Flowers III. It was now 75–65 with five minutes left.

In the next three and a half minutes, Wilson scored 8 points, while Flowers III added another basket to put the game out of reach at 85 to 72, with just under ninety seconds to play. Bradford hit another hanging jumper in the lane, and AJ sank 2 free throws to close out the game. Final score read 89–76. The win improved ACU to 12–3 in the GSAC at 24–3 overall. LPU slipped to 3–11 in conference play and 6–15 overall.

Twenty points, 4 steals, and 2 assists were the final numbers for AJ; Wilson added 19 points and 8 boards. "During the second half, I kept remembering what Coach Rutter had said at halftime about the starters stepping up," Wilson stated later. "I am so glad we were able to battle back and avoid the upset."

Flowers III had 12 points. Bradford and Bowers both had 7 points, while Gonzalez and Hayden each had 5 points.

LPU stayed with ACU for thirty-five minutes of the game. They were led by Austin Cook's 18 points. Leal-Cruz had 16; Ethan Galang and Jimmy Rodriguez both had 12 points.

The Firestorm has three conference games left, and all three are at home. ACU will battle first-place William Jessup University on Thursday at the Events Center.

CHAPTER 13

CHAMPIONSHIP FINISH

"I can do all things through Christ who strengthens me" (Philippians 4:13).

February 10, 2022
The Events Center
Glendale, Arizona
William Jessup University Warriors

The Firestorm had fought back all conference season long to stay in the GSAC title race, from being the preseason favorite to starting the conference season with one win and two losses. ACU found itself in a great position. With three games left in the conference regular season and clinging to second place, ACU would be home for the final three games with a chance to finish for at least a tie of the title, if the Firestorm can win out. "We put ourselves in a great situation, but there is still a lot of work left to be done," Coach Rutter admitted the week leading up to the game.

The "white-out" atmosphere inside the Events Center was an added bonus to playing a top-ten matchup in the NAIA. WJU entered the contest with a 12–2 conference record, while ACU was 11–3. A battle for first place was on the line. The Firestorm beat the Warriors a few weeks before in Rocklin, California. WJU was going to be without one of its top players, Myles Corey. Myles was the second-leading scorer for the Warriors, but he injured his knee in the previous game. He could be out for several weeks. Cash Williams would have to rally the troops to make up for the loss of Corey.

The Firestorm wasted little time to take an early lead with baskets by Davis and a three-pointer from Bradford. The Warriors cut the lead to 5–3 eighty seconds later, when Tim Strijaous hit a three-pointer.

A tip-in by Davis and a layup by Robby Wilson made it a 9–3 Firestorm lead four minutes into the game. For the next ten minutes of the game, ACU was able to maintain a small lead over the visiting Warriors.

After a Firestorm free throw by Flowers III at the 4:30 mark, Bryce Davis went to work on the offensive end, scoring 7 straight points, and he gave ACU the first double-digit lead of the game at 30–20. There were now ninety seconds before intermission.

After WJU's Cash Williams scored a layup with :27 left, AJ matched that layup as time expired to end the half with a 32-to-22 ACU lead.

The Firestorm defense did a fantastic job by holding the high-scoring Warriors to only 22 first-half points, and its leading scorer, Cash Williams, to 2 points. WJU shot only 30 percent from the floor in the half, while ACU shot 50 percent, with Davis going 6 for 6 from the floor and 13 points.

Cash Williams came out in the second half to score a quick 5 points for the Warriors. Robby Wilson responded with 5 points of his own for the Firestorm. With two minutes gone in the second half, ACU still maintained a ten-point lead at 37–27.

The Firestorm was able to keep a double-digit lead for the next five minutes with 2 baskets from Bowers and baskets from AJ and Wilson. With 13:11 on the clock, ACU was up 45–34.

After ACU's Dom Gonzalez connected on one of two free throws with eleven and a half minutes left, the home team was up 46–36. Neither team was able to score for the next two minutes.

Freshman Marcus Green broke the drought by scoring 5 points, and that pushed the lead to 51–39, with eight and a half minutes to play. ACU seemed to be in control of the game, but they could not relax because there was plenty of time for the Warriors to make a run.

Tarren Storey-Way and Cash Williams did their best to keep the game within reach, but a jumper by KeyVaughn Williams put the Firestorm up 15 at 62-47 with 4:22 to play.

A three-pointer and a layup by Storey-Way cut the lead to 10 points at 62 to 52 with 3:47. Xander Bowers responded with a three-pointer and a dunk to push the lead back to 15, with just over two minutes in the game of the week. Those 5 points by Bowers pretty much closed the door on a Warriors comeback, 67-52.

Cash Williams did manage to score 9 points in the last ninety seconds for WJU. Free throws by AJ and layups by Bradford, Key Williams, and AJ maintained a double-digit lead. When the final horn sounded, the Firestorm had 75, and WJU, 63.

ACU led from wire to wire; the win moved the Firestorm into first place in the GSAC at 13-3 and 25-3 overall. WJU dropped to 12-3 and 24-3. The Firestorm had a half-game lead over the Warriors, plus it held the tiebreaker over WJU.

"We did a great job defensively today against an outstanding team," a smiling Coach Jeff Rutter responded shortly after the game. "We were able to take control of the game early on and hold them off. It was a great offensive game for either team."

ACU had 48 points in the paint, while WJU had 28. The Firestorm held the Warriors to 34 percent shooting from the floor for the game and only 21 percent from deep. Story-Way led all scorers with 21, while Cash Williams had 19 for the day, with 17 coming in the second half.

Like all year long, the Firestorm had a balanced scoring attack; Davis finished with 13, AJ had 12 points and 8 rebounds, Bowers 11 points and 5 boards, Wilson 9 and 8, and Green and Key Williams had 8 points apiece. Micah Bradford finished with 7 points, 8 rebounds, and 4 assists. Bradford also worked hard on the defensive end, disrupting the guard play of the Warriors.

The Firestorm will have a short turn-around, with Menlo on the schedule for Saturday afternoon.

February 12, 2022
The Events Center
Glendale, Arizona
Menlo College Oaks

One down and two more games to go on this season-ending homestand. It took ACU sixteen league games to finally get to where all the GSAC coaches thought the Firestorm would be in the conference for 2021–2022—at the top. It had been a long and difficult journey. However, neither the journey nor the work were finished.

How would Coach Rutter's squad react to taking over first place in the conference title race just two days ago? Motivation was not going to be an issue with Menlo. This was the team that beat ACU in the middle of January on a last-second shot. ACU played poorly in the first half of that game. The

Firestorm regrouped and took a second half in that game, but ACU failed to close out the game. That gave Menlo the opportunity to win the game on a buzzer-beater to upset the Firestorm. A win against the Oaks this Saturday would keep ACU in first place in the league.

Unlike the game at Menlo, the Firestorm got off to a hot start as Dennis Flowers III scored a jumper and a layup to lift the home team to a 4–0 lead in the first two minutes of play.

A basket by Robby Wilson and three-pointers by Bowers and Wilson gave ACU a 12–7 lead, with just over fourteen minutes left in the half. The Oaks made back-to-back three-pointers to take a 13–12 lead.

That Menlo lead did not last long, as ACU went on an 11–0 scoring run. In the next two and a half minutes, two three-pointers by Dom Gonzalez, a three from Paul Hayden, and a dunk by Bryce Davis put the score at 23–13.

Meno cut into the deficit, and it was a six-point lead, ACU 37–31, with just over a minute until intermission. In the last minute of play, Menlo's Khalid Price hit a jumper, while Hayden and Gonzalez closed out the first half, scoring with three-point baskets. Gonzalez's coming with four seconds left in the half. ACU was up 43–33.

"Fellas, don't expect to shoot 60 percent from three-point range in the second half," Coach Rutter warned in the halftime locker room. "You worked hard to have a ten-point lead at the break, but you know as well as I do that this lead could disappear quickly if we do not defend!"

The red-hot-shooting Firestorm connected on ten of sixteen attempts from behind the arc for 62.5 percent in the first half. Menlo shot 5–10 (50%) from deep range in the opening half. ACU also had 12 assists and 5 turnovers after twenty minutes.

ACU responded, coming out of the locker, by scoring the first 9 points with baskets coming from AJ, 2 hoops from

Davis, and a three-pointer by Wilson. That increased the lead to 19 at 52–33. That was quite a start for the hot-shooting Firestorm. "With that sizzling second-half start," Robby Wilson later said, "I knew we were going to win this game."

After the Oaks cut the lead to 16 with 15:05 to play, the Firestorm went on another two-minute scoring binge by rattling off a 10–0 run and taking a commanding 68–42. Wilson had a jumper, Williams added 5 points, and Bowers had a three-pointer. Bowers added a dunk shortly after the scoring run off of a great pass from Williams. The ACU lead was now up to 28 at 72–44 with 11:20 to play.

The Firestorm offensive kept on humming on all cylinders as Flowers III hit a jumper and a three-pointer to balloon the lead to 32 at 77–45 with eight and a half left in this Saturday matinee.

Menlo was able to cut into the lead and make it a twenty-four-point game at 81–57, with three minutes left until the final horn.

ACU's reserve five man, Shaun Wahlstrom, was able to get the last 2 baskets for the Firestorm to bring the final score to ACU 85–57.

"We played really well on both ends of the court today," Coach Rutter stated after the victory. "Our guys were excited to get another shot at Menlo after our last game against them!"

The team did prove Coach Rutter wrong after halftime, as the Firestorm was able to shoot 15–24 for 62.5 percent for the game from long-range. The ACU bench outscored the Oaks bench 39 to 6. Bowers had 11 points, 3 blocks, and 3 boards. Gonzalez scored 9, going 3–4 behind the arc. Hayden had 8, Williams had 5, Wahlstrom 4, and Green 2. Flowers III led all scorers with 17 going 7–11 from the floor. Wilson added 13, going 5 of 5 from the floor and 3 of 3 from the line, and 5 boards. Davis had 9 points and 5 boards.

"This is the first time I have been part of a team to beat Menlo," Robby Wilson gladly professed. "We came out hot in the second half to give us a comfortable lead."

Menlo had three players in double digits: Parker Haven with 18 and 6 boards, N'Jai LeBlanc with 13, and Khalid Price with 12.

Two down and one more game to go to win back-to-back GSAC regular season championships. The Firestorm would get the chance to do that in seven days at home on Senior Day.

February 19, 2022
The Events Center
Glendale, Arizona
Ottawa University (OUAZ) Spirit

The Firestorm worked hard to go from a 3–2 GSAC record in December to be in a position to win the conference outright with a Saturday afternoon win against its rival from nearby Surprise, Arizona, the Spirit from Ottawa University. OUAZ entered the game in fourth place at 10–7 in the conference. ACU was 14–3 with a one-game lead over Hope and WJU.

Between the women's and men's games, five seniors were honored before a full house at the Events Center. "This was a bittersweet moment for me," Robby Wilson commented after the game. "I was just trying to soak it in and remember all the memories inside the Events Center."

"I just appreciated my family coming out from California," Daniels recalled. "Even though I did not see much game action, they showed up constantly out of love."

The seniors were introduced with family members. A short highlight video was shown for each player, and a large action picture was presented to each senior: Xander Bowers, Micah Bradford, Chris Daniels, Darius Goudeau, and Robby Wilson.

"We are really rolling now, and we wanted to send the seniors out with another conference championship," Flowers III shared. "This was a chance to show how we stayed together with such a rough start to the conference season."

OUAZ won the opening tip, and Kam Malbrough hit the first shot, a three-pointer, 11 seconds into the game. Dennis Flowers III and Bryce Davis each scored baskets to give the Firestorm an early 4–3, just a minute into the game.

Neither team was able to gain the upper hand in the early moments of the game. AJ was able to tie the score at 19 with a layup at the 8:08 mark in the half.

Dennis Flowers III went on to score the next 8 points for the Firestorm, including two three-pointers. ACU was up 27–22 with five minutes before halftime.

Kolten Hitt nailed a three to pull the Spirit within 1 point at 29–28 with 2:39 left.

ACU closed the half with 8 straight points, with a dunk from Bowers, free throws from Hayden and Williams, and a steal and layup by Williams. ACU gained some momentum going into the locker room with a 37–28 lead over the Spirit. Other than 12 turnovers by OUAZ, the rest of the halftime stats were pretty even.

To start the second half, Micah Bradford scored the first five points for ACU, while Kam Malbrough matched with his own five points for OUAZ. So, with seventeen minutes left in the game, the Firestorm still had a nine-point lead at 42–33.

A jumper by Davis and a layup from AJ stretched the ACU lead to 46–33 with fifteen and a half minutes to the final horn.

ACU was able to go up 15 on a sweet Alley-Oop pass from Williams to Bowers. Xander cut along the left baseline with twelve minutes left to gracefully put the score at 54–39.

The Spirit was not done yet. Back-to-back three-point baskets by Keshawn Bruner and Jayce Catchings cut the deficit to 9. Josiah De'laCerda added another basket with 10:14 left to cut the ACU lead to 54–47.

ACU's freshman, Marcus Green, stopped the scoring run thirty seconds later by hitting a deep three-pointer from the right wing to push the lead back to 10 points, 57–47.

The lead was cut to 5 after De'laCerda added 2 free throws and hit a three-pointer. It was now 57–52 with just eight minutes to play.

Flowers III and AJ fended off the comeback by both players scoring 4 points apiece in the next two minutes to extend the lead to 13 at 65–52.

OUAZ made one final attempt to close the gap. Another three-pointer by De'laCerda and free throws by Catchings cut the ACU lead to 9 at 68–59, with two and a half minutes on the clock.

The Firestorm went on a 9–0 scoring run to close out the game with a three-pointer and free throws coming from Wilson and a layup from AJ. ACU closed out the game in championship fashion, scoring on 10 of its last 12 possessions to leave the final score at 77–59, as GSAC regular season champs at 15–3.

After the handshake line with Ottawa, the players joined friends and family on the floor for a celebration. Championship t-shirts and baseball caps were handed out and worn by the players and staff as they climbed the ladder to cut down the net.

In the locker room after the game activities on the floor, Coach Rutter praised them for their effort and execution. "Proud of you guys and your efforts. You closed the game out like true champions! Let's enjoy this for a few days. Remember, we need to stay humble and hungry for Conference Tournament Week."

Coach Rutter then closed the team in prayer, with a few other players and coaches adding to the post-game prayer.

Once again, the Firestorm enjoyed a scoring balance with four players in double figures. The ACU bench outscored the opposition again; 24–7 was the margin in this championship game. Flowers III had 14 points, Davis 13 going 6–7 from the floor, AJ 12 with 5 assists, Bowers 10 with 7 rebounds,

Wilson 7 and 7, Bradford 7, and Williams 6 points with 4 helpers. ACU shot 53 percent from the field, 11–13 from the line, and had 17 assists.

De'laCerda had a game-high 17 points and 6 rebounds. Malbrough added 16, and Hitt finished with 10. The team shot 36 percent from the floor and 10–13 from the line, but the Spirit also had 19 turnovers.

After wrapping up the GSAC regular season conference five days earlier with an eighteen-point win over OUAZ, the Firestorm would be the number-one seed in the GSAC Conference Tournament. They would play the winner of the eighth and ninth seed game. Hope International in Fullerton, California, was selected as the host school for the Conference Tournament. In previous years, only the six top teams would qualify for this tournament. Due to COVID affecting some teams, the league officials agreed to allow all ten teams to compete this season. The top six teams received first-round byes, while #7 played #10 and #8 played #9.

In the final NAIA poll for the year, ACU was ranked fourth; Loyola of New Orleans was ranked number one. ACU had plenty of its team win conference accolades. Coach Rutter was named the GSAC Coach of the Year. Angelo Johnson was named the Defensive Conference Player of the Year in the GSAC and made First Team All-Conference. Robby Wilson also earned First Team All-Conference honors.

ACU was a winner in eighteen of its last nineteen games and ten straight. Westmont won its play-in game with Life Pacific. Westmont finished 16–13 overall and 5–13 in conference, including a recent upset over William Jessup that allowed ACU to win the conference championship outright. The Warriors split its two regular season games with ACU. The score of both those games were 82–80. Westmont is a much better team than what their record indicated. The Warriors lost many close games through the year and forfeited some games because of COVID and injuries. Westmont also added a Portland University transfer Cly Griffith Jr. at the semester.

Westmont was not a team to take lightly, plus they had Freshman of the Year Nate Meithof, who was averaging 17 points per game on the season and 25 points per game in the two games against ACU.

Senior Day with families

Robby Wilson celebrating GSAC championship

February 24, 2022
GSAC Quarterfinals
Darling Pavilion
Hope International
Fullerton, California
ACU versus Westmont Warriors

The top-seeded ACU Firestorm was the home team and wore the gray jerseys, while Westmont wore their maroon traveling jerseys. The game was scheduled to begin at 5:00 p.m. Pacific Time.

The quarterfinal game got off to a fast start as both teams scored on its first possession. Dennis Flowers III scored a layup on a backdoor cut, and Ajay Singh scored Westmont's first basket on a layup at the other end.

The teams traded baskets, and the score was tied at 10 when Micah Bradford connected on a layup with 14:39 to play in the first half. The score was tied at 16 again with just under ten minutes before half.

A free throw by Micah Bradford and a dunk by Bowers gave the Firestorm a 19–16 lead with just over nine minutes left before the break. The Warriors responded with a 10–3 run to take a 26–22 lead on a layup by Cly Griffith Jr. with 5:22 until intermission.

To close out the half, ACU outscored Westmont 8–3 to go into the locker room with a 30–29 advantage.

Nate Meithof scored for the Warriors twelve seconds into the second half to put Westmont up 31–30. One of two free throws by Flowers III tied the score at 31.

In the next five minutes, the Warriors took control of the game by going on an 18–4 run, with Ajay Singh pouring in 12 of those 18 points. This gave the Warriors a 49–35 lead with 14:24 on the clock.

A free throw by Bowers and a layup with twelve and a half minutes to play by Davis pulled ACU to within 11 points, 49–38.

The Warriors' Singh exploded for 7 points during a 9–2 scoring run and an eighteen-point lead, 58–40 with just under ten minutes in the quarterfinal contest. This would be the largest lead of the game.

The ACU defense now started to extend its defense with trapping and pressuring to change the pace of the game. Baskets by Williams and Flowers, and a free throw by Marcus Green, cut the lead to 13 at 58–45 with seven minutes left for a comeback.

A 7-to-2 run from Westmont stretched the lead back to 18 at 65–47 with three minutes left in this matchup. Time was running out for a Firestorm comeback miracle.

Three-pointers by ACU's Paul Hayden, AJ, and Dom Gonzalez cut the lead to 69–58 with 1:43 left. "It was desperation time, and AJ was finding us to hit long shots to put us in position to try to make a run," Paul Hayden conveyed. A dunk by Bowers off of a pass from AJ cut the lead to 9 at 69–60 with ninety seconds left.

Jalen Townsell connected on a layup shortly after the dunk to push the lead to 11 at 71–60. Meithof added 2 free throws with fifty-three seconds left to give the Warriors a 73–62 advantage.

Paul Hayden hit a 3 for ACU to cut the lead to 8 with forty-five seconds left. After a steal by the Firestorm, Dom Gonzalez had a three-pointer rim out with fourteen seconds left. That ended any hope of a comeback win.

Westmont did it. They upset the top-seeded Firestorm 75–63. It was a slow and disappointing walk back to the locker room. Instead of preparing for the semifinals the next day, the team would be traveling back to Arizona early on Friday.

"We knew Westmont at full-strength is a national tournament team, so we were expecting a battle," commented Coach Rutter after the loss. "We came out in the second half slow. Westmont got to the rim too easily. We also turned the ball over 6 of 8 possessions, and Westmont was able to take advantage of that. Our response was not what I expected. Our guys tried to do too much individually instead of relying on each other, and the deficit grew."

ACU had not lost a game in six weeks. "Perhaps it is a humbling moment to emphasize how much we need to rely on each other, especially in times of adversity," Coach Rutter concluded.

"We needed to be humbled again," Robby Wilson said after the game. "We need to lean on each other. So far, after every loss this season, we have bounced back better. I fully expect our guys to do that again."

Dennis Flowers III echoed that message, "This setback was monumental because it put a chip on our shoulder. Another chance for us to pull together for the national tournament."

Ajay Singh led all scorers with 21 points, Meithof added 17, and Jared Brown had 11. The Warriors shot 52 percent from the floor and scored 15 points off of 10 ACU turnovers.

"As a staff and as a team, we are so proud of the improvement we have seen in the last week," said Westmont Coach Landon Boucher. "We look like a completely different team from a month ago."

Dennis Flowers III had 13 points and 3 steals; AJ had 10 points and 3 assists; Davis had 9; Hayden 8; and Bowers had 7 points, 9 boards, and three steals. For the game, ACU shot 37 percent from the floor, 9–18 from the free throw line. With its early exit from the GSAC conference tournament, The Firestorm will have several weeks to rest and prepare for the NAIA national tournament on March 10.

CHAPTER 14

NATIONAL TOURNAMENT

"Ah, Sovereign Lord, You have made the heavens and the earth by Your great power and outstretched arm. Nothing is too hard for You" (Jeremiah. 32:17).

February 28, 2022

After having Saturday and Sunday off, the Firestorm returned to practice on Monday.

The first item of this practice was a briefing from Coach Rutter on the upcoming NAIA tournament. Coach informed us that, unfortunately, Arizona Christian was not selected to host the opening-round games. ACU facilities do not meet all the NAIA requirements to be a host site. According to Coach's contacts, ACU should be a number-one seed at a regional site. Everything is speculation now, but the Firestorm could be sent to Texas, Wichita, or maybe Louisiana. The selection show will be on Thursday evening; then we will know. Whatever happens, we should be a number-one seed on the road and may need to face a number-two seed on their home court.

Coach Rutter then assigned the players to focus on three things individually for the rest of the season. The three items they need to work on are a basketball skill, a sacrifice they will make, and a Bible scripture that fits them personally.

March 1, 2022

The coaching staff was assigned to meet with their four players and check in with them on the skill, sacrifice, and scripture.

The team then stretched and warmed up. The practice focused on transition defense and making good decisions on offense. The practice ended up with the three-on-three shell defensive drill in which the players on defense needed to get three defensive stops in a row.

March 2, 2022

It was a day off of team practice, but some players requested individual work-outs with coaches. Coach Rutter spent time watching the Westmont defeat with the guards and another time with the bigs.

March 3, 2022

The team returned to the Events Center after practice to watch the Selection Show for the NAIA tournament. ACU was selected as a number-one seed in the Cramer Quadrant and for a regional site and the fourth-overall seed out of sixty-four teams. Arizona Christian would face Tougaloo College of Mississippi in one semifinal of the opening round. Southeastern University of Lakeview, Florida will be the host site. Southeastern will play Xavier of Louisiana in the other semifinal.

March 4, 2022

Practice was at 9:00 a.m. on Friday. ACU does not hold classes on Friday. The practice did not get off to a good start. Several players were late. One of the team's standards for the season was showing up ten minutes early for any team function. This was not met, and the whole team had to run sprints. If one player did not finish the sprint workout in the desired time, the whole team had to run again. It was surprising that some of our players were not in as good a shape as they should have been at this point of the season. So there was some extra running for the team before practice even started.

Shortly after practice, the team loaded into vehicles to drive to St. Mary's Food Pantry in Phoenix to do its second service project for the season. Our team was scheduled to work from 11:00 a.m. to 1:30 p.m. Half the team worked on bagging fruit while the other half helped load cars at this drive-through food bank. It was interesting to see the players, managers, and coaches work together for a wonderful cause. It was also encouraging to see how most of the players interacted with each other, other volunteers, and those receiving the donated food. "I was working with Darius, Chris, and Xander outside, loading the vehicles with food," Paul Hayden recalled. "We were off campus, and we were doing an activity that had nothing to do with basketball or a class. It was a nice break! Plus, we knew we were serving others."

March 5, 2022

Since the team did not play a game in over a week, the coaches arranged for an alumni scrimmage to be played on this late Saturday morning. The first half saw the Firestorm win 48–30. The first five starters failed to move the ball crisply and turned the ball over 8 times. The players also over-dribbled the ball. The second half saw the alumni win 48–41. This was a beneficial scrimmage, since it showed that the team needed a little brush-up on the offense movement and importance of spacing. The team would have Sunday off.

March 7, 2022

During the day, Coach Rutter was able to spend some time during the day with individuals to review the tape from the Saturday alumni scrimmage. The school was on Spring Break, so we practiced at 1:00 p.m. instead of our normal time slot of 3:00 p.m. At practice, there was a lot of 5-on-0 offensive work to work on spacing, no dribbling, cutting, and ball movement. The players seemed to appreciate the extra review of the offense in preparation for teams that the Firestorm had not played all year.

March 8, 2022

It was a travel day to Tampa, Florida. Half the team had a direct flight to Tampa while the other part of the team had a layover in Dallas. The teams for the opening round games were all at the Sheraton in Tampa/Brandon. It was over a thirty-minute drive to the Southeastern campus in Lakeland.

The team was able to get to Southeastern late at night to get some shooting in on the floor. "It was exciting for me to be back in Florida for the tournament," AJ admitted. "It would allow my family to come and see me play again."

March 9, 2022

After going for an early lunch, the team went to the Polk County Natural Reserve to see all sorts of wildlife. The players got to view alligators from a safe distance, raccoons, and many different kinds of birds. "It seemed like we were in another country." Hayden stated after viewing all the wildlife in Florida. When our two-hour stay at the nature reserve was over, we went to practice at Southeastern.

March 10, 2022

There was a morning film session, and then the team went to grab lunch. There was a lot of downtime in the afternoon. The team meal was at a BBQ restaurant, and the team was going to have a later practice to coincide with our game time on Friday.

March 11, 2022

It was game day—a day that the players waited for all year and a day that seemed a long way off after the loss in the conference quarter finals. There was another scouting session on Tougaloo to go over personnel and offensive and defensive concepts.

Paul Hayden (also known by his teammates as AP for Apostle Paul) led a team devotional time in the late afternoon. Paul used the story from John 5 and the invalid of thirty-eight years trying to get into the healing pool at Bethesda. The disabled man could never make it into the pool, but one day, Jesus healed the man and changed his life forever. Christ changed the man's physical and spiritual life. "This is one of my favorite stories in the Bible," Paul confessed. "This man was looking in the wrong place for the answer. Today, we focus on winning, fame, and fortune as the answers to life and happiness. Our focus needs to be on Christ; He is the true answer for joy, now and for all eternity."

To lighten the mood before the first tournament game, Coach Welty showed a video that he had assembled of "Not-so-Top-Ten" highlights from the year. Needless to say, hearty laughter burst out while viewing the mishaps in practice or games. To the surprise of no one, Shaun Wahlstrom and Robby Wilson took home the honors of "Most Blooper Appearances"!

NAIA Opening Game
Southeastern University
Lakeland, Florida
The Furnace Gymnasium
#1 seed ACU versus #16 seed Tougaloo
College Bobcats

After over a two-week layoff from its last game, The #1-seeded ACU Firestorm was set to face the #16-seeded Tougaloo Bulldogs from Jackson, Mississippi.

In the opening game, #8 Southeastern was defeated by #9 Xavier of Louisiana, 57 to 56. Xavier would play the winner between ACU and Tougaloo on Saturday evening.

The scouting report heading into Friday night's game reported that the Bulldogs had two really quick-scoring guards, and one really active big man. They also have a tendency to put lots of pressure on the ball.

Neither team was able to score on its first possession, but Flowers III scored the first basket of the game, while Micah Bradford completed a three-point play to give the Firestorm the early lead at 5–0.

ACU found itself with a ten-point lead with just over thirteen minutes left after Bowers scored on a layup to give the Firestorm a 16–6 advantage. On two different occasions, ACU was able to take an eleven-point lead, the last coming off of a Robby Wilson basket to make the score 25–14, with 8:18 before half.

The Bulldogs' Cameron Woodall led a 14-to-4 scoring run by scoring 6 points. That brought ACU's lead to 1 point, 29–28 with just under four minutes before the break.

The Firestorm regained the momentum heading into the locker room by closing out the half with an 11–4 run, with AJ scoring 6 points and Gonzalez hitting a 3 with twenty-three seconds left in the half and a 40–32 lead.

At halftime, ACU held an 18–10 lead with rebounds. ACU had 10 assists compared to 1 assist for Tougaloo. ACU shot 56 percent from the floor, while the Bulldogs shot 42 percent in the half. Copeland led all scorers with 14 points for Tougaloo.

Dennis Flowers III started the second half as a scoring machine by contributing 7 of the 7 points that the Firestorm managed to put on the board in the first three minutes of play. That extended the lead to 49–34. The Firestorm continued to build on the lead with baskets coming from AJ and Williams, and a dunk by Davis. ACU now had a twenty-point lead, 57–37, with just over fourteen minutes to the final horn.

For the next eight minutes of play, the Firestorm was able to maintain a lead around the twenty-point margin. Davis added 5 of those points and baskets coming from several teammates, including 2 free throws from Williams at the 6:51 mark that pushed the lead to 21 at 72–51.

Darryl Jones and Copeland tried to lead a big comeback for the Bulldogs, but the closest they got was a thirteen-point deficit. KeyVaughn Williams scored the final basket of the night to bring the score to 76–61.

ACU was able to win the opening game and advance to Saturday's regional final.

"We got off to a great start defensively to take control of the game. Dennis did a nice job on Copeland in the second half to really make him work for everything," commented Coach Rutter after the win. "AJ and KeyVaughn did a nice job of controlling the game the rest of the way. Saturday will be a great matchup. Xavier is elite defensively, and we will have to be patient and work for great shots."

AJ and Williams both had 14 points, with AJ recording 6 assists, and Williams, 3 helpers.

Flowers and Davis both had 11 points. The team shot 57 percent from the floor and 83 percent from the free throw line, making 10 of 12.

Tougaloo was led by Woodall's 18 points; Copeland was held to 3 second-half points and 17 for the game. The Bulldogs shot 38 percent from the floor and only 58 percent from the line by going 10 of 17. The Bulldogs finished the year at 21 and 9.

March 12, 2022
Southeastern University
Lakeland, Florida
The Furnace Gymnasium
#1 seed ACU Firestorm
#9 Xavier University of
Louisiana Gold Rush
NAIA Regional Final

The pregame devotions were from Romans 8:35–39: "Whatever hardships, danger, or situations life throws at us, we are more than conquerors through Christ that loves us. Nothing can separate us from God's love."

"The word 'conquerors' really caught my attention in this passage," Robby Wilson admitted. "That applies to life *and* in basketball games."

In this second-round NAIA Regional Final, ninth-seeded Xavier Gold Rush would square off against the number-one seeded and fourth-ranked Arizona Christian University. The winner of this contest would advance to the round of 16 in Kansas City. Xavier's defense is one of the best in the nation. ACU ranks in the top ten in both defense and offense. Xavier entered the game with a 23 and 6 record, while ACU was 28 and 4.

The game got off to a blazing start as Dennis Flowers III scored an uncontested layup off of the tip. Two–zero, five seconds into the game.

Ninety seconds later, Cory Wells nailed a three-pointer for Xavier to give the Gold Rush a 3–2 lead.

Bryce Davis and Robby Wilson made the next two baskets of the game, giving ACU a 6–2 lead. The basket by Wilson gave him 1,000 career points at ACU. Wilson is the sixth player in the program's history to record over 1,000 points and grab 500 rebounds.

A basket by Xavier's Cameron Wells and a layup and dunk by Xander Bowers put ACU up 10–5, with 13:35 before the half.

The teams battled evenly for the next six minutes. At the 6:35 mark, Robby Wilson hit a three-pointer to give the Firestorm its biggest lead of 8 and 24–16.

Led by Richard Makye's 6 points and Nigel Allen's 5 points, the Gold Rush finished the half on a 17–5 run. This gave Xavier a 33-to-29-point lead at the half.

The halftime stats showed both teams shooting just a little better than 40 percent from the floor. Xavier led the rebounding battle 19–12 with 7 of those rebounds being offensive. ACU turned the ball only 3 times, and Xavier had 6.

Even though The Gold Rush gained momentum heading into the locker room, there was no panic in the Firestorm during halftime. Coach Rutter's message was the same during most halftimes throughout the season. "Continue to be solid in half-court defense, box out and rebound, be patient on offense, and work for great shots."

At halftime of the Xavier game, Bowers added later, "I remembered what I had said to the team before the tournament started. I will do everything in my power to not let any of you guys feel like we did after last season's loss."

Makye continued his hot scoring to start the second half, as he scored the first 5 points of the half. That put the Gold Rush up 38–29 with just over eighteen minutes left in the regional final.

ACU needed to make something happen to regain the momentum. The Firestorm was able to erase the nine-point deficit quickly as AJ hit back-to-back three-pointers, and Wilson followed with hitting back-to-back threes. In a matter of two minutes, the Firestorm went from down 9 points, 38–29, to up 1 at 41–40 with a 12-to-2 run. "When I saw Robby hit those three-pointers," Shaun Wahlstrom remembered, "that gave me great satisfaction, knowing that I had helped prepare Robby for that moment." Wahlstrom battled against Wilson every day in practice. All the momentum built by the Gold Rush going into halftime and early in the second half evaporated with the ACU three-point assault!

The team, including the bench, were rejuvenated. This now had the making of a seesaw battle until the final buzzer. ACU was able to open up a five-point lead at 49–44 on a nifty drive and layup by Key Williams with 10:24 to play. "Xavier had smaller guards on me, and I was able to get into the paint and score or distribute the ball to an open team-mate," Williams stated after the game.

The teams traded baskets for the next five minutes with the ACU lead staying in the three- to six-point range.

ACU was up 57–53 with 5:35 left in the game and a ticket to Kansas City on the line. AJ's three-pointer off of a pass from Williams gave ACU a 60–53 with 4:19 left to play.

Flowers III hit 2 free throws, and AJ cashed in another jumper to lift the

Firestorm to an eleven-point advantage at 64–53, with just over three minutes to play.

Makye hit a three-pointer for Xavier to cut the lead to 8 with 2:24 left.

Bowers then threw down an offensive rebound dunk off a miss by Flowers III to push the ACU lead to double digits at 66–56 with 1:47 left to the final buzzer. "Xander Bowers altered the game on both ends," a smiling Paul Hayden reported after the game. "I knew this team could go far with Xander playing that way!" The trip to Kansas City was now becoming more of a reality, with time running out for the Gold Rush.

Ten seconds later, Cameron Wells hit a two-point basket to cut the lead back to 8.

As the shot clock was winding down with just over a minute to play, Dom Gonzalez made a tough shot with his left hand in the lane. He was fouled while shooting, and the ball dramatically hung on the rim—and finally dropped in. The Firestorm bench erupted into jubilant celebration. Gonzalez calmly went to the line and buried the free throw, which extended the lead to 11. That pretty-much sealed the deal and a trip to KC for ACU.

Nigel Allen made 5 free throws for Xavier in the last minute of play, while Flowers III went six-for-six from the line for ACU. The final score was ACU 75–63.

After losing in the Regional Final round in 2021 to Carroll of Montana, the Firestorm gathered for a short celebration and trophy presentation on the floor. The sting of last year's loss was over. The Firestorm was headed to Kansas for the round of 16.

"I am so proud of how tough the guys were tonight," a joyous Coach Rutter commented after the win. "We played well for much of the first half, but Xavier went on a 13–5 run to finish the half. We challenged the team to fight for everything, and they were amazing in the second half. Xavier is statistically the best defensive team in the country. To score 46 points in a half with 65 percent shooting is significant."

AJ led a balanced scoring attack for the Firestorm with 16 points. Flowers III added 14 points going 8 for 8 from the line. Bowers went 6 for 7 from the floor for 11 points with 7 boards and 4 blocked shots. The 4 blocked shots made Bowers the all-time career leader with blocked shots at ACU.

"Xander Bowers was so special tonight," Wilson complimented his teammate. "He was dominant on both ends of the floor." Wilson ended the night with 11 points and 5 boards. Williams assisted on 7 baskets and had 4 points. ACU improved to 29 and 4 on the year. "It was win or go home for our seniors. We were not going to exit early like we did last season," a smiling KeyVaughn Williams added after the big win.

The next game will be on Thursday in Kansas City against Bethel College of Kansas.

Xavier was led by Makye with 18 points, Allen with 13, and Wells with 10 points and 7 boards. The Gold Rush ended the year with a 23 and 7 record.

After the handshake line with Xavier, the Firestorm players gathered for fist bumps, hugs, and lots of smiles and laughter. There was a short trophy presentation for the NAIA Regional Championship. A few minutes later, the team arranged itself for a quick photo opportunity, and then the team made its way to the locker room.

Coach Rutter praised the team, and several players chimed in with comments.

Team Captain Robby Wilson shared, "Hey, we were down half, but I kept thinking of the word 'conquerors' from the devotions earlier today from Romans Chapter 8. Conquerors are what we needed to be in the second half, and we were!"

Coach Rutter closed our team meeting, and then told us some players needed to get tested for COVID before we left the Southeastern campus.

"As we left the gym that night," AJ remembered, "it was satisfying, but we knew we would enjoy it for twenty-four hours. Then, it was getting to Kansas City to continue on our journey."

One would think this would be a big time for celebration. It was for the players at Olive Garden, but not for the coaches. The coaches were scrambling with booking flights to Kansas City and locating rental vans once we got there. "If there is a will and a credit card, there is a way," Coach Welty recalled about booking flights for KC. Coaches were also making calls to get some information on our first opponent in KC, Bethel College of Kansas.

Coach Rutter had his own dilemma. He had planned to fly back to Phoenix to attend a surprise birthday party that he planned for his wife, Kristin. His first flight was canceled, and he had to scramble to make connections so he could get back to the Southwest in time for the birthday party on Sunday.

To make a long story short, by Sunday night, the team made it to Kansas City on two different flights. Coach Rutter made it back to Phoenix for the birthday party for

Kristin. Yes, she was surprised that Coach came to Phoenix before heading to KC. Coach and the entire Rutter family flew out to the National Tournament site on Monday.

CHAPTER 15

KANSAS CITY–BOUND

"I have fought the good fight, I have finished the race, I have kept the faith" (2 Timothy 4:7).

While in Kansas City:

Kansas City means BBQ. Yes, our team ate at several restaurants, where most of the team enjoyed some of Kansas City's finest BBQ. "Coach V., I recommend the burnt-ends sandwich here," Coach Welty suggested at one of our stops. Coach Welty grew up in the KC area, so he was well-aware of what was tasty. The entree did not disappoint, as some team members took the advice and enjoyed a burnt-ends BBQ sandwich for the first time.

The Firestorm team and many other teams for the tournament stayed at the Crowne Plaza right across the street from the Municipal Auditorium. It was a convenient location to be able to walk to many eateries and food markets. "Our team was so focused on this entire trip," Paul Hayden reflected later on. "We had a quiet confidence that we would find a way to play well and advance to the next game."

The sixteen teams at the NAIA tournament all had designated times to practice at the old Kemper Arena, which is now Hy-Vee Center. In 2017–2018, the facility was converted from a nineteen-thousand-seat arena to a two-level youth sports and community gymnasium. From 1975–1993, Kemper Arena actually hosted the NAIA national finals.

Two times during their stay in Kansas City, Coach Welty's parents, Keith and Valerie, hosted the ACU basketball team for dinner. The Weltys lived about fifteen minutes away from the hotel. After feasting on delicious food, the team was able to relax by watching television, playing Ping-Pong, and spending time somewhere other than a hotel. Before leaving one night, the Weltys gave each player and coach a bag full of treats. What a nice surprise to be enjoyed for the next few days!

The NAIA developed a program that local Kansas City businesses can sponsor a team for the tournament. It is a wonderful opportunity for the KC area to host and connect with teams that come from around the country. Great Western Bank sponsored the Firestorm, and Doug Goumer and R.D. Hilt, representatives from the bank, were a part of our team for our entire stay. They were in the locker room before and after games, and they sat with our team on the bench. Doug and R.D. showed Midwestern hospitality and treated the team to an excellent meal one evening at the Yard House restaurant, just down the street from our hotel.

Several times during our stay, players walked a few blocks from the hotel to the College Basketball Experience, located in the Power and Light District in downtown KC. It is a large, two-story, fan-interactive facility connected to the T-Mobile Center. The players enjoyed competing against each other with the dynamic exhibits that challenged their basketball skills. The National Collegiate Basketball Hall of Fame is also located within the College Basketball Experience building.

Many players took advantage of attending the team devotions that were held almost every day of our trip to Florida and KC. "It was because of the devotions on the trip and the messages that Coach Chambers shared with the team throughout the season that I, finally, was able to play free. I gave the Lord control of my identity," Robby Wilson admitted.

"What was special about our devotional time on the road trip was that more and more players were showing up for the optional player- or coach-led devotional meetings," Hayden observed.

On Wednesday, the day before the competition started, for the devotional time, Coach Welty organized a prayer walk at the Memorial Auditorium. Coach Welty explained, "A prayer walk is having people walk outside around a building or inside a room and pray out loud or silently. There were five players and coaches who walked the block around the auditorium on a dark and dreary day in KC. Inside, there were four walking around the area between the lower and upper bowl of the auditorium. When the prayer walk was done, Robby and Paul spent some time in prayer on center court. "We were praying for safety for all the teams, God's will to be done, and that we would play for Christ," Hayden concluded.

March 17, 2022
NAIA Round of 16
Municipal Auditorium
Kansas City, Missouri
4th-Ranked ACU versus. 20th-Ranked
Bethel College Threshers
(North Newton, Kansas)

Municipal Auditorium has been the site for the NAIA national tournament for many years. This facility also hosted several NCAA Division 1 Final Fours in the 1950s and 1960s. John Wooden's first UCLA title was won in this building back in 1964.

"We were glad this day finally came," AJ reflected back. "The team was just happy to play again on such a nice, shiny floor and the glare of the bright lights."

When the players were in the locker room, getting ready for the game, Coach Welty walked in with a surprise guest. It was Coach Karvis, ACU's strength and conditioning coach. Coach Karvis trains several teams for ACU, so he will attend home games.

"You really made the trip?" Xander Bowers questioned.

"That was the deal I made with several players! You advance to KC, and I will be there," an excited Coach Karvis responded.

Bethel College is about two and a half hours southwest of Kansas City, so they had about three hundred or so fans in the stands. Meanwhile, ACU had some family members and alumni in attendance at the game, which tipped off at 5:30 Central Time.

"We knew that Bethel had an outstanding player in Jaylon Scott," noted Xander Bowers. "I was going to be matched up against him the majority of the game, but I knew one player was not going to beat us."

The Threshers won the opening tip, and Jaylon Scott scored fifteen seconds into the game with a twelve-foot jumper. AJ gave the Firestorm its first lead of the game a minute later with a three-point basket for a 3–2 lead.

Five points by Bethel's Harper Jonas and a layup from ACU's Bryce Davis left the Threshers holding on to a 7–5 lead. Robby Wilson tied the score at 7–7 with a layup, with 17:31 left to play in the half.

ACU was able to build a small lead with three-pointers coming from AJ and Bradford, but a jumper by Bethel's Clifford Byrd II re-tied the score at 13 at the 14:11 mark. The Firestorm then went on an 8–0 scoring run in the next ninety seconds with 5 points from Davis and a three-pointer from Paul Hayden: 21–13 ACU.

Bethel's Scott scored 4 straight to cut the lead to 4 at 21–17. Davis hit 2 free throws to put a stop to the small run to make the new score 23–17 with just over eleven minutes to play in the half. "My primary focus in this game was defensive end," Davis stated later. "Part of my assignment was to try to slow down Jaylen Scott, one of the best players in the country."

During the next three and a half minutes, three-pointers from AJ and Flowers III, free throws from Flowers III, and a layup by Bradford pushed the lead to 9 at 33 to 24. Things were looking good for the Firestorm, but, as in the past, ACU struggled to finish out the half with the momentum.

Bethel finished the end of the first half with a 16–7 run. Bryant Mocaby scored 8 of those points, and Jaylen Scott nailed a three-pointer as time expired in the first half to lift Bethel to a 40–37 advantage.

There was no panic in the Firestorm locker room, since the team had grown accustomed to this situation throughout the season. "I played a sloppy first half," Bowers admitted. "I picked up some ticky-tack fouls, and that bothered me. Some uplifting and positive words from my teammates picked me up. They had my back, and I would have theirs in the second half."

The halftime statistics were pretty even for the teams. Both teams were shooting in the mid-40-percent range from the floor; rebound numbers, turnovers, assists, and personal fouls were all close. "We have been down before at halftime," Wilson reacted to the Bethel run before intermission. "We needed to lean on our previous experiences!"

Bethel extended its lead to 5 with another basket by Scott in the first minute of play in the second half. Flowers III hit back-to-back baskets to cut the lead to 4 at 42–41. Scott hit one of two free throws to put the Threshers up 43–41.

Wilson tied the score at 43 with a layup with 16:18 left in this round of 16 matchup. Micah Bradford put the Firestorm on its next possession with a three-pointer and a 46–43 lead, with just under sixteen minutes left.

ACU was able to stretch the lead to 6, 51–45 with a steal and a layup from KeyVaughn Williams with just over thirteen minutes to play.

The ACU lead was still 6 at 55–49 with 10:38 on the clock, when Flowers III, Wilson, and Darius Goudeau all connected from long range in less than a minute to put the Firestorm in control at 64–51.

ACU was able to keep a double-digit lead for the next four minutes of play. The lead expanded to 14 on a tip-in from Bowers. Flowers III followed that up with a layup to push the lead to 16 points at 73–57. There was now just over five minutes left in the game and a trip to the quarterfinal round.

The Threshers were able to cut the lead to 10 after Clifford Byrd II connected on a layup with just under two minutes to the final horn.

ACU was able to close out the scoring with Xander Bowers scoring a layup and Williams adding 2 layups in the closing minute to give the Firestorm an 82–66 victory and a spot in the quarterfinal round on Saturday.

Jaylen Scott led all scorers with 21 points and 18 rebounds. He later would be named as a NAIA first team All-American. Bryant Mocaby finished with 11 points. Bethel struggled from the free throw line, going 7 of 17 for 41 percent. The ACU defense also limited Bethel to 1 of 16, 6.3 percent, shooting from long range in the second half after allowing 6 threes in the opening half.

Bethel finished the 2021–2022 campaign at 28–7.

Five players scored in double figures for the winning team. Flowers III had 16 with 3 assists. "Playing under the bright lights in this arena is something I really thrive on," a jubilant Flowers III announced. AJ had 14 points and 3 helpers, Wilson had 11 points with 13 rebounds, and Bradford had 10 points and played outstanding defense on Bethel's shooters. Bowers had foul trouble in the first half but finished with 10 points and 8 rebounds in eighteen minutes of action. Davis had 9 points and 9 rebounds. "Winning this game was very satisfying," Davis added. The ACU bench outscored the Threshers 22 to 16. The Firestorm shot 46 percent from long range at 11 of 24 and out-rebounded Bethel 46 to 40.

Shortly after the game, Coach Rutter had these comments: "Bethel is very talented offensively, and we did a great job defensively tonight. Flowers III and Bradford were very good for us tonight on the defensive end. We did not close the half as well as we would have liked. Bethel did a nice job of converting from our turnovers. We played a better second half with AJ and Xander Bowers hitting some real big shots to help us close out the game."

"Micah Bradford was special against the Bethel shooters," Robby Wilson added. "They had a difficult time getting space to get their shots, which frustrated them."

ACU improved to 30 and 4 on the year and will play in the quarterfinals on Saturday afternoon.

The team celebrated advancing to the quarterfinals by enjoying a team dinner for BBQ at Jack Stack.

March 19, 2022
Municipal Auditorium
Kansas City, Missouri
NAIA Quarterfinals
4th-ranked ACU versus 13th-ranked
William Jessup University Warriors

Facing the challenge of beating GSAC rival William Jessup for the third time in one season was going to be a tough task. "Our coaches had a good scouting report on Jessup," AJ added. "We knew what we needed to do, but we needed to execute the plan." Arizona Christian would need to compete against a team that was playing at full strength. Myles Corey was back in the lineup for the Warriors. Corey had injured his knee several weeks ago and did not play against the Firestorm when the teams met in February. However, he had played in the three previous games for WJU with a large brace supporting his knee.

WJU got off to a quick start by taking an early 6–1 in the first two minutes of this quarterfinal game. ACU's Bryce Davis scored the next 4 points to pull the Firestorm to within 1 at 6–5. "Bryce was really getting into a great rhythm during the tournament if he could avoid getting in early foul trouble," Flowers III observed.

A 7-to-2 scoring run lifted the Warriors to a 12–point lead. Baskets by Davis and Bradford allowed ACU to stay in the game. Tarren Storey-Way made 2 free throws to give WJU a 19–11 advantage with 10:44 before intermission.

Robby Wilson scored the next 5 points in the next twenty-four seconds to pull the Firestorm to within 5 at 21–16. The teams battled evenly for the next few minutes.

That is when ACU went on a 7–1 scoring run with AJ scoring 5 points and Darius Goudeau's offensive rebound put back to cut the deficit to 2 at 25–23.

A three-pointer by Dom Gonzalez and a layup from AJ tied the score at 30 with just over five minutes before the break. The teams saw the lead seesaw back and forth for the next few minutes. WJU's Myles Corey hit a jumper with 42 seconds left in the half to tie the score at 38.

ACU was able to retake the lead going into halftime as AJ nailed a three-pointer with four ticks left on the clock. ACU's 41–38 halftime lead gave the Firestorm some momentum at the halfway point of the game.

Back in the locker room at halftime, Coach Rutter reminded the team that several key WJU players were battling foul trouble in the first half. The team did not need to be reminded that the Warriors would battle hard for the next twenty minutes. The winner of this game would advance to the national semifinals. The halftime stats showed ACU with a huge advantage with rebounds 24 to 7, with Wilson grabbing 7 of those. Both teams shot around 48 percent from the floor. ACU had 9 turnovers, while WJU only had 4.

After an ACU turnover and a missed three-pointer by WJU, Bryce Davis scored a layup with 19:04 to play to build the lead to

43–38. "Our games against WJU are always exciting and fast-paced," Davis recognized. "Scoring efficiently in the paint is a big way for me to help our team." The Warriors responded with 5 straight points to tie the score at 43 with just under eighteen minutes to play.

Micah Bradford then completed a three-point play, and Wilson converted a layup to build an ACU five-point lead at 48–43. The teams exchanged baskets for the next two minutes. Tarren Storey-Way hit a shot from deep to tie the score at 54 with 14:29 left.

The next four minutes saw little scoring by either team, but WJU got three-point buckets from Corey and Storey-Way to take a 60–56 lead with ten and a half minutes to play.

Xander Bowers responded for ACU with back-to-back baskets to tie the score at 60, which started a 10–0 run for the Firestorm. Davis added a dunk and a jumper, while Bowers added another basket to give ACU a 66–60 advantage with 7:22 on the clock.

Myles Corey put a stop to the ACU run by connecting from deep. Bowers answered that with a dunk that fueled a 12-to-2 run for the Firestorm and a 78–65 lead. AJ scored 6 points during that stretch and added a nifty assist to Davis on a well-executed pick and roll on the left lane line. That left just over three minutes left on the clock. Would the Firestorm be able to withhold one last push from the Warriors in the waning minutes of the contest?

The deficit was cut to 9 points two different times down the stretch. ACU was able to go 10–12 from the free throw line, and Williams added a layup to give the Firestorm a 90-to-79 victory over William Jessup. ACU was headed to the national semifinals on Monday night for the first time in the program's history.

ACU became the first GSAC team to advance to the NAIA semifinals since 2014–2015, when the GSAC had two teams in the semifinals.

"They played so hard and executed what we asked them to do," Coach Rutter stated after ACU's thirty-first win of the year. "AJ showed, once again, that he is as good as any point guard in the country; he was solid on both ends. Dennis did a great job on Cash Williams defensively (Williams: 12 points). Micah Bradford did a nice job on their other shooters. Our effort in the first half was good, but we turned the ball over often, which hurt us, with WJU scoring in transition. Jessup was tough today, and they had a great season!"

The Warriors finished the year 30–7. They were led by Tim Strijaous's 28 points. Myles Corey had 14, Storey-Way had 13, and Williams had 12. Malik Corey was the only player that scored coming off the bench with 9 points.

"We knew it was going to take a lot to beat them (WJU) a third time in a year," Robby Wilson added after the game. "We were confident and stayed humble, which has been our theme for the tournament. Having an

All-American point guard, AJ, was also a boost to our confidence."

Arizona Christian had a balanced scoring attack, with four players scoring in double figures and the bench scoring 29 points. Angelo Johnson (AJ) finished with 22 points, going 3 of 4 from long range and 5–5 from the line. He also had 3 assists. "This was a big step for our program," AJ commented after the game. "Making it to the national semifinals is special."

Davis had 16 points, going 7 of 8 from the floor. Wilson had another double-double with 11 and 12. Bowers added 14 points and 7 boards, while Williams finished with 8 points. Flowers III and Bradford both scored 6 points each, but their sticky defense only allowed Cash Williams 12 and Jordan Adams 3 points.

The rebounding battle belonged to ACU 46–26, and point in the paint saw the Firestorm with a huge 62-to-32 advantage.

The team will be back in action on Monday night with a national semifinal matchup with the second-ranked and top-seeded team of the tournament, Loyola of New Orleans.

March 21, 2022
NAIA National Semifinals
Municipal Auditorium
Kansas City, Missouri
4th-ranked ACU versus 2nd-ranked Loyola
University of New Orleans Wolfpack

The NAIA National Semifinals were set to take place at Municipal Auditorium in Kansas City. Game 1 featured two #1-seeded teams, with Loyola University at 35–1 ranked #2 on the year-end poll versus Arizona Christian at 31–4, also ranked 4th. "Loyola is by far the toughest scout that I had all year," Coach Welty confessed. "They are the best team we will play. Loyola's length, athleticism, and zone defense was a concern entering the game."

Loyola was coming off of a quarterfinal win over the College of Idaho, while ACU beat William Jessup.

Final team huddle before semifinal game

The Firestorm only had one full day to prepare for the long and athletic team that thrived on pressuring and forcing turnovers. As a team, they averaged turning teams over 18 times a game.

ACU won the opening tip, but six-teen seconds into the game, ACU had its first turnover. An offensive charging foul was whistled against Bryce Davis. Loyola responded by scoring the first 6 points of the game; 2 were from Myles Burns and 4 from Zach Wrightsil.

Davis got the Firestorm on the board with a jumper with 17:08 to play in the opening half, 6–2 Loyola. The Wolfpack opened up an 11–4 lead after Burns connected from deep and added a layup at the fifteen-minute mark.

Dom Gonzalez and Paul Hayden both hit from long range to pull the Firestorm within 3 at 13–10 with just under thir-teen minutes in the half. After ACU's Dom Gonzalez rimmed out a three-pointer thirty seconds later to potentially tie the score, Jalen Galloway hit a three to put the Wolfpack up 16–10.

A layup by AJ and a dunk by Davis pulled the Firestorm to within 2 at 16–14. There was still 9:35 before the break.

The Wolfpack went on an eleven-point run with 3 straight possessions scoring three-point baskets. Two long-range shots came from Cameron Dumas and one from Galloway. Galloway also added a two-point hoop. Loyola was taking control of the game at 30–16 with just under six to play before half.

Davis scored another basket to momentarily break the Wolfpack run. ACU was down 30–18. Six more straight points from LU made it a 36–18 lead. ACU had its work cut out for it with 4:13 to intermission time. ACU did mount a little comeback with a six-point run of its own, with Bowers scoring 5 of those points. It was now a twelve-point deficit with 1:46 left until the Firestorm could regroup.

Loyola's Fava drilled a three to make the score 39–24. However, a basket by Davis and 2 free throws by Patrick Fisher in the final minute left the halftime score at 39–28 Loyola.

Loyola's trapping defense and 1-3-1 half-court zone defense had caused 7 ACU turnovers. ACU was losing the rebounding battle 15–21. "Loyola's defense dictated our offense, and we struggled getting space to shoot tonight," Dennis Flowers III stated. Shooting 2 of 11 from behind the arc for 18 percent was not going to cut it for ACU. Davis had 10 points at half and Bowers had 5. That was over half of ACU's output for the first twenty minutes. LU's Galloway led all scorers with 12 points.

The Wolfpack was shooting 43 percent from long range at 6 of 14.

The Wolfpack started the first three minutes of the second half with an 8–2 scoring run and a 47–30 lead. LU continued to take control of the semifinal game, as the lead was stretched to 54–34 with just over thirteen minutes left in the game. ACU had an uphill battle, but there was still time left for a comeback.

Bryce Davis tried his best as he scored 5 straight points to make the score 54–37 with 12:15 to play. After the game, Davis proclaimed, "I was more excited than nervous for this game. Loyola is an excellent team." LU's Zach Wrightsil matched Davis's 5 points by scoring 5 straight of his own to return the Wolfpack lead to 20 at 59–39. Myles Burns was able to give the Wolfpack its largest lead of the night by hitting a three-pointer with 8:21 left to put LU up 66–43.

ACU made some progress with cutting into the large deficit. Scoring was coming from Hayden, Darius Goudeau, AJ, and Flowers III. It was still a fourteen-point lead for Loyola, 77–63, with 1:12 left before the final horn.

Two free throws by AJ with eleven ticks left of the clock pulled the Firestorm to within 10 at 80–70, but Galloway slammed home the last 2 points of the game with eight seconds left. The 82–70 victory advanced the Wolfpack into Tuesday night's championship game.

Kansas City–Bound

Xander Bowers in KC

Coach Rutter and DG

All American AJ

Frustrating game for ACU and Key Williams

Bryce Davis made All Tournament Team

*Team Captain Robby Wilson Vocal Leader
on and off the floor*

Dennis Flowers III in KC

Team Huddle late in game

It was a silent ACU locker room for several minutes before Coach Rutter addressed the team. There were players with heads buried into towels. Some were openly crying. Others just stared at the carpeted floor. It is never easy having a basketball season come to an end. Basketball is a six-month season, so friendships and strong relationships are built within the team. This team grew so close together with spending two weeks on the road in Florida for the opening round weekend games and in KC for three games.

The team had some optional team devotional times during the last two weeks on the road, which helped strengthen the Christian bond between players and coaches.

Coach congratulated the players on a wonderful season and for their fighting spirit in tonight's tough battle. Players were given the chance to share thanks or words of advice with one another. There were certainly plenty of tears and reflections. It seems the further a team advances in a tournament, the more difficult it is to see the tournament run end.

Finally, Coach Rutter thanked the five seniors for their leadership and hard work. They put the ACU program on a new level. Instead of Coach Rutter closing in prayer, like he did before and after every game, he opened it up for anyone wanting to pray to do so. Several players and coaches contributed to the prayer time. Coach Welty closed the prayer and then asked the team to join him in praying the Lord's Prayer.

One last team breakdown for the 2021–2022 season was led by captain Robby Wilson. Then, the moment most players struggle with—taking the jersey off for the last time—extremely difficult for the seniors. "It shattered me to take off the ACU jersey for the last time," Robby Wilson recalled. Nothing seemed to go our way against an excellent team. The better team won tonight. They have so many veterans on their team."

"Credit to Loyola," Coach Rutter complimented after the game. "They played a great game, and they are very good. Loyola never let us get into a rhythm offensively. We had some good looks early, but we just did not hit them."

"Loyola does such a nice job of converting offensive rebounds and turnovers. We gave up a few too many of them to keep us in striking distance."

Coach Rutter continued, "It is disappointing because we really believed that we had a good chance at winning the tournament. This group has been such a great team to coach. Tremendous growth on and off the court. Our seniors, Robby Wilson, Xander Bowers, Darius Goudeau, Micah Bradford, and Chris Daniels, were special and elevated our program. Unbelievable teammates. They will be tough to replace."

Looking to the future, Coach Rutter made these observations, "We have a great group returning for next season, so we expect to compete for the title again."

Loyola had five players in double figures, with Wrightsil leading the way with

20 points and 9 boards. Burns had 16 and 9, Galloway 16 and 8. Dumas added 12 and Fava with 10.

ACU had 16 turnovers for the game and out-rebounded LU 44–41. The Firestorm only shot 19 percent from behind the arc at 5 of 27, 36 percent from the floor, 19 of 23, 83 percent from the line.

Bryce Davis had 19 points with 9 boards. "I was determined to display my very best effort tonight," Davis commented. "It is disappointing; we could not get the win." Flowers III added 15, Hayden 13 points. AJ was held to 7 points with 4 assists, Goudeau had 6 points and 6 boards, and Bowers had 5 and 5.

The Firestorm ended the year at 31 and 5. Bryce Davis was selected for the All-Tournament Team. Davis shared, "Making the All-Tournament team is just a reflection of my amazing teammates and dedicated coaches that helped me play confidently in the tournament,"

Loyola did win the NAIA Championship the following night.

The following day, the Firestorm team members flew back to Phoenix on two different flights. Both flights had KC Royals baseball fans flying down for spring training games. The players needed to resume in-person classes on campus. It is a difficult transition from basketball six days a week to a few weeks off from the game. As the days go by, the pain of the end of the season turns into thankfulness of experiencing a year to remember *for such a time as this.*

AFTERTHOUGHTS

Megan Vetter: "When we arrived in Kansas City, I was happy for my own reasons, but watching the team experience nationals as a whole was so rewarding. It is like watching the world through the eyes of your children. This team was special! They put in the work on and off the court, in the weight room, in the athletic training room, to make sure they were prepared to play to the best of their abilities. This was proven by their phenomenal run all the way to the semifinals for the first time in the university's history."

Coach Ray Karvis: "I will always cherish this season as special. We try to run the strength center like a D1 program, but we aren't as available for games, as we train multiple teams early in the morning. I'm very appreciative of the coaching staff for including me as 'part of the family.' It was so great to be able to lead the team in a dynamic warmup at the Sunday practice before the Monday semifinal game. Talking with the players during our time in KC and being by the bench during the games was thrilling. The experience at Kansas City will always be one of great treasure. To know that, as their strength coach, I could help them achieve their goals.

"Coach Rutter was a big part of DST being at ACU. Man, we are grateful for that, and what we are doing with what we call a championship culture."

Robby Wilson played three seasons at ACU. "I am going to miss the battles in practice and games, the relationships with players and coaches. It was a great time to be a Firestorm during this time, being able to help the basketball program take some big steps forward in its development. ACU may not be for everyone, but for me, I grew so much in so many areas of my life—especially in my spiritual walk. ACU is certainly a transformational university."

Dennis Flowers finished his first season with ACU after playing at Carroll College of Montana, and he played in several games last season in Kansas City. "My transition to joining the ACU program went better than I anticipated. The players and coaches were really welcoming. It took me a few days after our loss to Loyola to process it all. It was amazing to see how new players and coaches this season were able to come together. Our season is an example of what buying into a team and system looks like. It took some time, but it happened!"

Chris Daniels played for two seasons at ACU and graduated in May of 2022. He is currently working and studying for the LSAT exam to enter law school. Chris's role on the team was to play on the scout squad, which prepared the Firestorm for upcoming opponents. Daniels stated, "My role on the team was definitely hard, so I tried to keep an attitude of gratitude and humility. Be thankful for what I have instead of what I don't. I would have struggled with this role if I was younger, but I could handle it being older and more mature. I genuinely didn't care for my own success. This group of guys was so close!"

Paul Hayden finished his second season at ACU. "It took for a while to let it sink in that the season was over. We were able to build such deep relationships throughout the season with our long road trips. We will miss Robby's strong work ethic and his leadership capabilities. I could play, knowing that he always had my back."

Bryce Davis just finished his first full season with ACU. "I loved playing in Kansas City and the atmosphere of this tournament. We got to participate in games played at a high level. I was glad we got to fight together until the end with teammates and coaches."

Xander Bowers played three seasons at ACU. "The early part of the season was tough on me. I had to battle a few minor injuries, and the uncertainty if I was going to play the season or redshirt. If it wasn't for my close friends and teammates, especially Darius and Chris, I don't know if I would have been able to keep a cool head through the rough start of the season I had." Xander is looking at some different opportunities to play basketball professionally overseas.

Shaun Wahlstrom just finished his third season with the ACU basketball program. He redshirted the 2020–2021 season. "The basketball season is such a long season. When looking back on our journey, it seemed like it went so fast. Kansas City was great! The two weeks away for the NAIA tournament allowed our team to bond together. We were able to experience so much as a team and support each other. It wasn't easy, but I learned to accept my role on this team. It was satisfying watching Bryce, Robby, and Xander have success on the court. Competing against these guys every day prepared them for the games. Also, I enjoyed encouraging guys on the bench during games when things were not going well.

"Once we returned from KC, I didn't have a lot of time to dwell on the basketball season. I had to start track practice in a few days and get ready for a Saturday track meet." Wahlstrom throws discus and shot put for the Firestorm.

Angelo Johnson (AJ) just completed his second season at ACU. "It was such a great experience to go through the entire season with these guys. We went to battle together and had a great season. Playing in Kansas City was special. The bright lights, new basketballs, and shiny court made it a wonderful experience. It didn't take me long to get over the loss to Loyola. I was ready to get back to work."

Coach Welty: "I loved coaching each of our seniors this year. Each one of those guys has a special place in my heart for their hard work, buy-in, and energy they brought each day to practice. There is nothing like playing in Municipal in March. I'll leave it at that. It is a special place!"

Coach Oetjen: "The national tournament was a ton of fun. This was a special team. We played 11–12 deep sometimes, which is not very common. Our depth played a huge part in making it to the final four. AJ, BD, Rob, Dennis made plays. Key, Dom, Paul, Xander were faithful and clutch in key moments. I'll never forget this team, how competitive they were; they wanted to do it for each other."

WHAT ABOUT YOU?

During your lifetime on Earth, you will make thousands of decisions. Those decisions will affect what will happen to you while on this planet. However, there is only one decision during your earthly existence that will determine where you will spend eternity. The biggest decision that you will ever make is: what do you do with Jesus Christ? Jesus said, "I am the way, the truth, and the life. No one comes to the Father except through me" (John 14:6). We can't buy or earn our way into heaven, and there are no grandchildren in heaven. It is a free gift for all! Sometimes, traditions and religions complicate the simple, free gift of salvation. A valuable lesson can be learned by one of the criminals that was crucified next to Jesus. In his last hours of life, the criminal requested, "Jesus, remember me when you come into Your kingdom."

Jesus replied, "I tell you the truth; today you will be with me in paradise" (Luke 23:42–43).

Many of you who have read this book are sports fans. Players, coaches, and fans like to be on the winning side. If you are on

Jesus's team, you are guaranteed to have the final victory—victory over death. You will leave this earth as a winner and get to celebrate for all eternity! "For God so loved the world that he gave His only Son, that whoever believes in Him should not perish but have eternal life" (John 3:16).

Becoming a follower of Jesus is as simple as the ABCs:

Admit *you're a sinner.* Romans 3:23 says, "For all have sinned and fall short of the glory of God."

Believe *Jesus died for your sins and still lives today.* Acts 16:31 says, "Believe in the Lord Jesus, and you will be saved."

Confess *that He is your Savior and your Lord.* Romans 10:9 reads, "If you confess with your mouth 'Jesus is Lord,' and believe in your heart that God raised Him from the dead, you will be saved."

Once you make that decision to be a Christ follower, tell another Christian that you trust so they can help you take the next steps.

WHAT ABOUT ME?

If God can use me, a kid who grew up on a small dairy farm in Wisconsin, He can use anyone to share His love and good news of eternal life.

Faith is like a credit or bank card; we do not know what is in our possession until we actually activate it! Your faith has the potential of limitless provision and protection. *Activate it!*

Now, from Numbers 6:24–26,

May the Lord bless you and keep you;
May the Lord make His face shine
   upon you
and be gracious to you;
May the Lord turn His face toward you
and give you peace.

ABOUT THE AUTHOR

For Such a Time as This is Jack Vande Zande's first book. Early in his professional years, Vande Zande wrote sports and news stories during his radio broadcasting career. He also did play-by-play announcing, which helped with writing this book.

Vande Zande taught middle school English for over twenty years and has coached basketball for over thirty years at several different levels.

He and his dear wife, Carrie, live in Sun City, Arizona. Their two children live in Wisconsin.